SENSE

&

NONSENSE!

The World as Seen Through
A Prism of Many Colors!

Boyè Lafayette De Mente

Two things are infinite;
the universe
and human stupidity;
and I'm not sure
about the universe!

—*Albert Einstein*—

—HUMAN BEHAVIOR EXPOSED!—

SENSE

&

NONSENSE!

Male Dominance, Ignorance
Religions & Willful Stupidity

The Abuse of Human Sexuality,
Tribalism, Territorialism, Race,
Color, Religions & Self-Interest

Boyé Lafayette De Mente

PHOENIX BOOKS/PUBLISHERS

Other Books by the Author
Available from Amazon

[Books on China]

The Chinese Mind—Understanding Traditional Chinese Beliefs and Their Influence on Contemporary Culture

Chinese Etiquette & Ethics in Business

China's Cultural Code Words [Key Terms that Reveal the Culture and Mindset of the Chinese]

Chinese in Plain English

Survival Chinese

Instant Chinese

Etiquette Guide to China—Know the Rules That Make the Difference

[Books on Japan]

Japanese Etiquette & Ethics in Business

KATA—The Key to Understanding & Dealing with the Japanese

Japan's Cultural Code Words

The Japanese Have a Word for It!

Mistress-Keeping in Japan—The Pitfalls And the Pleasures

Exotic Japan—The Sensual & Visual Pleasures

Discovering Cultural Japan

Business Guide to Japan

Japanese in Plain English

Survival Japanese & Instant Japanese

Speak Japanese Today—A Little Language Goes a Long Way!

Instant Japanese
Survival Japanese
Japan Made Easy—All You Need
to Know to Enjoy Japan
Dining Guide to Japan
Shopping Guide to Japan
Etiquette Guide to Japan—Know the
Rules That Make the Difference
The Japanese Samurai Code—Classic
Strategies for Success
Japan Unmasked—The Character & Culture
of the Japanese
Elements of Japanese Design—Understanding
& Using Japan's Classic *Wabi-Sabi-Shibui* Concepts
Sex and the Japanese—The Sensual Side of Japan
Samurai Strategies—42 Secret Martial Arts from
Musashi's "Book of Five Rings"
Why the Japanese are a Superior People—The
Advantages of Using Both Sides of Your Brain!
Amazing Japan—Why Japan is one of the
World's Most Intriguing Countries
Exotic Japan—The Sensual & Visual Pleasures
SABURO—The Saga of a Teenage Samurai in
17th Century Japan

[Books on Korea]
Korean Business Etiquette
Korean in Plain English
Korea's Business & Cultural Code Words
Etiquette Guide to Korea— Know the Rules
That Make the Difference
Instant Korean
Survival Korean

[Books on Mexico]

Why Mexicans Think & Behave the Way
They Do—
The Cultural Factors that Created the Character
& Personality of the Mexican People
Mexican Cultural Code Words [hard-cover]
There's a Word for It in Mexico [paperback]

[Other Titles]

Which Side of Your Brain Am I Talking To? –
The Advantages of Using Both Sides
of Your Brain
How to Measure the Sexuality of Men
& Women By Their Facial Features
Samurai Principles & Practices that will Help
Preteens & Teens in School, Sports, Social
Activities & Choosing Careers
Romantic Hawaii—Sun, Sand, Surf & Sex
Romantic Mexico—The Image & the Realities
Women of the Orient
Asian Face Reading—Unlock the Secrets
Hidden in the Human Face
Why Ignorance, Stupidity and Violence
Plague Mankind
How to Measure the Sexuality of Men
& Women by Their Facial Features
Bridging Cultural Barriers in China, Japan,
Korea & Mexico
EROS' REVENGE—Brave New World
of American Sex!
ONCE A FOOL—From Japan to Alaska by
Amphibious Jeep

[Books on Arizona]

Amazing Arizona—Fascinating Facts,
Legends & Tall Tales
Visitor's Guide to Arizona's Indian Reservations
The Grand Canyon Answer Book—Everything
You Might Want to Know and Then Some!
Cultural Code Words of the Hopi People—
Key Terms that Reveal the History, Heart,
Traditional Customs & Wisdom of the Hopis,
including their incredible prophecies
Cultural Code Words of the Navajo People—
Key Terms that Reveal the History, Heart,
Traditional Customs & Wisdom of the Navajos

***Some of the above titles are also available in
Chinese, Czech, French, German, Hebrew, Italian,
Indonesian, Japanese, Polish, Portuguese,
Russian and Spanish.*

CHAPTERS

The Ongoing Perversity of Human Males!

The Ongoing Perversity Of Human Males

Throughout human history there have always been elements of ignorance and stupidity in the mindset and behavior of males that have inflicted incredible violence and suffering on most of mankind since day one.

Deep-seated beliefs that grew out of selfish interests, tribalism, territorialism, race, skin color, and religions have so divided human beings—again particularly males—that still today these factors are major elements in all areas of life.

In many males these six elements, separately or combined, override logic, objectivity and rationality in both subtle and obvious ways, resulting in behavior that is negative instead of positive, disruptive instead of harmonizing and destructive instead of constructive.

Examples of irrational, illogical and harmful behavior are so deeply ingrained in the minds of many males that they have become institutionalized and ritualized in customs and laws and have persisted since the dawn of human history because the essential mindset of males has not changed and people with invested interests in the customs and laws have made sure that they continue to survive.

Men Are Animals / Women Are Angels
Homo sapiens are indisputably members of the animal kingdom notwithstanding the fact that as

many as one-third or more of all members of humanity deny that relationship.

The taxonomic designation of modern man as *homo sapiens* literally means "thinking man"—or to be more politically correct "thinking human being," since women are definitely members of the same species—but this designation is, in fact, questionable.

Given the history of mankind and today's current events, it appears that the label *homo sapiens* is more often wrong than right. But to be fair, it is only a small portion of humanity that gives human beings a bad name—that small portion that destroys and tortures and kills in a way not seen in the rest of the animal kingdom.

And this alone should be enough for those who deny the animals origins of humanity and claim a divine creation to step back and ponder the implications of their beliefs. It takes an awful lot of rationalizing to explain away the inhumanity of large numbers of human males whom no benign loving god would create, or put up with.

Most people, including those who claim a divine origin for mankind (even with all of our blemishes and faults) *do* recognize and admit that in the lower order of animals (if you can *get* lower than human beings!), male-female relationships have historically been con-trolled by the biggest and strongest males in whatever group was concerned.

These big strong male animals are typically referred to (by professionals who study such things) as alpha males—which is something like "first males" (as in "first lady" when referring to the wife of a president), since "alpha" means the "first" of anything."

And again despite the classification of humans as *homo sapiens* and despite any claims of a divine origin for mankind, from the dawn of humanity it was alpha males who made the rules, got first choice of the females and often kept exclusive rights to as many of them as possible.

One good thing that evolving societies did—and was picked up on by the Christian religion—was ruling that males should have only one wife.

Civilization Puts a Kink
In the Sex Life of Males

As said, civilization finally put a kink in the sexual monopoly of big strong males. After the advent of larger organized societies most men, officially at least, had to limit themselves to just one mate at a time, but in most societies males made sure they still had access to mistresses, concubines, harems and prostitutes.

Then along came Judaism, Christianity and Islam— all of which were created and controlled by men and all of which established "god-given" laws controlling the sexual behavior of men and women, with the laws naturally skewered in favor of men. In these male-created and controlled religions, females were a male after-thought created to serve men.

As time went by, overly zealous Christian popes and theologians—all males and often men who didn't like women—began to preach that women were naturally evil and would seduce and debase men if they had the slightest opportunity. They then created a world in which women had to deny and suppress their sexuality, resulting in indescribable frustration and suffering to the point that mental and physical ailments among women became common.

And in Moslem societies the ruling clerics (in the name of "God," of course), sanctioned the primitive alpha male concept of sexual behavior, allowing men to have several wives and to treat women in general as inferior shadows, to be covered and concealed from the eyes or presence of males not members of their families.

What all of the ancient world's alpha males and all of the religious clerics, ministers, popes, priests, shamans—or whatever they are called—misunderstood or ignored was the fundamental sexual nature of human beings.

These misguided and id/ego-driven men denied or ignored the fact that among all members of the animal kingdom, including human beings, sexuality comes right after survival in the built-in gene-powered drive. Furthermore, male humans, unlike some of our lower-order relatives, are "in heat" virtually all the time. The only time they are not is after they have exhausted all of their sex energy. Females, on the other hand, want sex only on certain occasions and with selected males.

If Gods Were Actually in Charge!
If gods were actually in charge of human nature and had any control over human behavior you certainly would not expect them to complicate their respon-

13

sibility by making men and women so sexual...and then allow their Earthly agents to create extraordinary barriers designed to *prevent* men and women from engaging in sex at will...even labeling sex a mortal sin except under carefully prescribed circumstances that favored men!

No matter which way or how often this male-designed world is white-washed it is both irrational and in-human.

Of course, there were enough valid social and political reasons for male leaders of early societies and religions to curb the sexual behavior of men and women. But the way they went about it was both inhuman and cruel. First of all, they put most of the responsibility on women, accusing them of not being able to control their sexual nature and therefore being a clear and present danger to society.

Throughout the history of Jewish, Christian, Islamic and other male-controlled societies virtually all women have been forced to suppress their natural sexuality to a degree that left them frustrated and subject to a variety of physical and mental ailments. In more modern times these ailments have been diagnosed by men as being caused by "female hysteria."

Despite the "sexual emancipation" of women that began in the United States in the early 20th century, picked up speed in the 1950s and now often appears to be moving at the speed of light, most American women still today are constrained in their sexual behavior, repressing, ignoring or denying their sexuality to a significant degree.

Female attitudes toward sex and their sexual behavior derive, of course, from religious concepts that were created by men ages ago and ever since have been interpreted by males and enforced by men with physical force as well as the threat of social and spiritual sanctions.

With the "power of God" in their hands, male religious leaders long ago succeeded in brainwashing most women to not only accept the sexual restrictions placed on their behavior, but to also become firm believers in the righteousness of the laws—written and unwritten—that controlled their sex lives.

Of course, this male position did not originally derive from any divine source. It was nothing more than a way for men to control the sexual behavior of all females in their group or tribe.

Because males were controlled by their animalistic instincts they did not want other males to have sexual access to the females around them—and like lower animals they were driven to mate with as many females as possible in an unconscious urge to have off-spring.

Another factor in the male compulsion to control the sexual behavior of women was their very early recognition that females are far more sexually potent than males—that women can engage in sex several times a day every day and not be the worse for wear, while even the most masculine males are incapable of—or are not interested in—having sex more than two or three times a day—and usually not every day.

This reality, plus the fact that completion of the sex act temporarily weakens males leaving them more vulnerable, may have engendered a deep-seated fear in the subconscious of all males that resulted in them wanting and needing to control females.

In any event, the male fear of female sexuality has historically resulted in the vast majority of females being forced to suppress and deny their nature.

Even after the advent of civilization and the appearance of husband-wife relationships, the duplicity of the male mind resulted in them coming up with a variety of ways to have carnal contact with women other than their wives. These ploys ranged from secondary wives and concubines to harems and access to prostitutes.

The first appearance of virtually true sexual equality between men and women in the United States occurred in the 1950s as part of the so-called hippie movement that started in San Francisco, California.

Among a significant portion of this group young women were free to have as many sexual partners as they wanted. Some male hippies made a point of offering their girl friends to their male buddies—and discovered that it was a real turn-on for all of them.

The Cultural Revolution Goes On
The male-dominated business, political and religious institutions that have traditionally molded and controlled the mindset and behavior of people are losing their hold on humanity because of cultural changes and technology that is exposing their abuse and misuse of power to the public at large, making it

possible for ordinary people to make their own decisions.

Television, with all of its good and bad elements, has become the new family, the new church, and the new school room of humanity. The stupidity, the perfidy, and the inhumanity that is shown in unending broadcasts from around the world is so shocking that the innate goodness in most of humanity that has long been ignored, oppressed and impotent—except in case of revolutions brought on by mass rebellions—is finally beginning to make itself felt through nonviolent means, with more sexual references and sexual activity being major elements.

In the U.S. one of the institutions that the new phenomenon of mass visual and verbal communication has revealed as virtually bankrupt is the political party system of government that is often based on the influence of self-interest and money. The weaknesses and failings of this system are so obvious they don't have to be named.

Members of the system will not reform it. That will take the combined voice and actions of an enlightened and courageous public.

Other institutions whose power over the beliefs and behavior of people is waning rapidly is that of large institutionalized and ritualized religions, particularly those that are cults in the true sense of the term— especially god-based religions such as Judaism, Christianity and Islam...the only large cult religions that have significant power in controlling the mindset and influencing the behavior of masses of people.*

---

*A cult is, and I quote from Webster: "A system or community of religious worship and ritual, especially one focusing on a single deity or spirit; obsessive devotion or veneration for a person, principle or ideal." Christianity is a perfect example of a cult.

But as long as these religions provide a rationale for the inhuman and irrational behavior of people, along with virtually freeing them from being responsible for their actions, the bulk of humanity cannot become rational in mindset or behavior.

Incredibly, there have been ancient religions that got the nature of human beings and our physical, emotional and spiritual connection with the cosmos mostly right. These have included, in part, Shintō in Japan and the religious concepts of several of America's Indian tribes.

But these religions have been isolated, generally regarded as primitive and/or savage and ignored by the new monotheistic, aggressive and militaristic religions that emerged in the Middle East and Europe. Still today the only long-term hope for humanity is a set of universal beliefs that reflect the true female-male nature of life as well as the cosmos at large, and encourages mankind to continue the long struggle to escaped its primitive id-based past and finally achieve the full potential of the human race.

In the right hands, the new audio, visual and com-munications devices, despite their obvious negative elements, can be the means by which this will happen because initially only neutral technology is capable of usurping the power and influence of irrational, in-human cultures.

There is already encouraging evidence of a growing number of males and females utilizing the Internet to advance the cause of humanity, but this number is far from reaching the tipping point and the irrational elements in all cultures continue to have a death-grip on the minds and behavior of the majority of people.

Boyé Lafayette De Mente

[1]
Why God-Based Religions
Have Failed!

Throughout human history most of mankind has depended more or less upon religions [spiritual beliefs]—or to be more exact, shamans and other religious leaders—to create, teach and enforce behavioral standards in all areas of life.

These standards were designed to control the beliefs and actions of people. But it is, of course, a given that religions have never been successful as creators or arbiters of a truly humane and fair morality.

Religions, particularly Judaism, Christianity and Islam have, in fact, been the source of much of the immorality that has plagued the Western and mid-Eastern hemispheres of the planet since their inception. You might say that after men created God in their own male image everything went to Hell!

It is no doubt true that Judaism, Christianity and Islam were founded with the best of intentions but it was not long before they were turned into instruments of discrimination, oppression, violence and murder. Throughout their history discrimination and war have been one of their primary legacies to mankind.

Over the millennia the vast majority of people who have accepted and attempted to live by the precepts of these three religions—in other words, to live morally upright lives according to the precepts of their particular religion—have been the least power-ful, the most down-trodden and the most victimized by the state and by the church—with the vast majority of them naturally being females. And because these religions were founded and ruled by men they were designed to favor males and to oppress females...all in the name of an omnipotent male God.

The word God itself has been turned into a catchall term that is used to justify murder by individuals and mass-killing by states. Pathological killers as well as the most upright members of societies beseech God to aid them in the destruction of their competitors and enemies, and praise God when they succeed.

That this incongruity is ignored by many of those who profess to believe in and follow the precepts of a "loving God" is pathological to the extreme. To be more precise, it is a form of insanity. In virtually the same breath "God the Creator and Savior" becomes "God the Avenger, the Destroyer and the Bringer of Death" to one's enemies and disbelievers.

In human history good and bad have never existed in reality as fixed polar opposites. They have always been circumstantial and were whatever was pre-scribed at the time by the ruling powers—the clergy, the government and the military; or whichever one of these entities was dominant. These three institutions have also traditionally worked hand-in-hand to indoctrinate, subjugate and control people for their own purposes.

It goes without saying that for the vast majority of people survival and some degree of security and com-fort take precedence over all other things. And if professing to believe in something like Islam, for example, will provide this security and comfort, even to a small degree, many people programmed in that faith will willingly believe and obey even the most irrational and inhuman dogma.

Many in all of these faiths, however, pretend to believe only because the religions have powerful sanctions at their disposal to force people to go through the motions of belief and obedience. These sanctions include the threat of eternal punishment in Hell, exile from the Church, social disgrace, and—historically in some cultures and still today in others—arrest, imprisonment, torture and execution.

When the United States was founded some of the teachings of Christianity that are humane, positive and nurturing were incorporated into the laws of the land. But institutionalized Christianity was not made a state religion because it was clearly seen by the founders as an enemy of intellectual and personal freedom. They knew firsthand that state religions soon degenerate into oppressive regimes.

And yet, despite the good intentions of the American Constitution and the Bill of Rights, the men who made up the power structure of American society continued to engaged in discrimination of all kinds; against females, non-Caucasians and especially black slaves and the original inhabitants of the Americas who were regarded as sub-human without rights, to be subjugated and confined or eliminated altogether. The latter "solution" was actively promoted on a state and local government level for some two centuries. Several American states as well as northern Mexican states bordering the U.S. paid bounties for the scalps of hunted down and murdered Indian men, women and children.

Early Americans in one New England state also had smallpox infected blankets delivered to Indian tribes in their vicinity in ongoing attempts to exterminate them. So much for the ballyhooed "all men are created equal and have the right to life, liberty and the pursuit of happiness" concept of the Founding Fathers!

Where Religions Have Gone Wrong

It goes without saying that people in God-oriented societies typically behave in ways that are contrary to religious teachings. In many cases this is because the teachings range from being impractical to inhuman, dangerous or worse, and following them makes no sense.

The concept that the "Kingdom of Heaven" is *within the individual*—not in some after-death place high in the sky—is probably the most important of all of the insights attributed to the biblical Jesus, but it has been down-played or ignored by all levels of God-based religions. In fact, according to the teachings of Christianity you can "sin" left and right and still go to Heaven if you confess and accept Jesus as your savior before you die. That is an incredible copout that has equally incredible power over the minds of the brain-washed masses.

Nothing in the world is more dangerous than sincere ignorance and conscientious stupidity!

—*Martin Luther King Jr.*—

In more ways than one the God-based moralities of Judaism, Christianity and Islam have become an unfunny joke.

The daily news is rife with references to God that are so irrational they go beyond being ridiculous. Clerics, preachers, terrorists, politicians, military men and others are constantly calling on God to bless them and their countries, and to bring death and destruction to their enemies.

There are far more damaging mental and moral aberrations across the board in societies where the guidelines for human behavior are based on an irrational male-oriented theological concept—with so-called entertainment being one of the most conspicuous examples.

It is incredible that modern-day entertainment—one of the biggest and most culturally influential of all industries—is more often than not based on catering to the most primitive, savage and gross side of humanity. The Christian Church in particular cannot compete with this form of mass cultural conditioning.

In fact, the Bill of Rights attached to the American Constitution forbids both the government and religious institutions from interfering with the public expression of the most gross and dehumanizing elements of "freedom of speech."

This morass of immorality has come about because over the decades the laws of the United States have been skewered by politicians under pressure from academics, business leaders and others to favor and permit the debasement of humanity—and most people at large accept this situation for a variety of reasons: they tell themselves they can't change it; that it is not their responsibility, and so on. It is also no doubt true that many people who publicly oppose this pandemic of cultural sleaze are strongly attracted to it.

The goal in producing and marketing sleaze is, of course, to make a profit. And the reason it is so profitable is because the attempts of religions and secular societies to control human behavior, despite their good intentions, have created a hunger for sleaze in all of its forms...especially those that are sex-related. Feeding this hunger drives the behavior of the bulk of humanity.

As I have noted before making a profit is the new morality...even though high-tech is the new small god of morality for some—meaning anything goes.

The Human Need for a Spiritual Dimension

In the first place, Judaism, Christianity and Islam have never had all of the right answers for humanity—spiritual or otherwise—as history has so graphically demonstrated.

I am not saying that spirituality is out. In fact, spirituality is *in*, including among a growing number of Americans. But more and more so-called Christians and non-Christians alike are creating their own personal paths to fulfilling their spiritual needs—generally based on spiritual insights and wisdom that developed ages ago before and outside of Judaism, Christianity and Islam.

And then, of course, some two-thirds of the world's population is *not* Christian or Jew—even if in name only. These are the Muslims, the Buddhists, the Hindus, and so on—most of whom have had good reason for disliking and fearing Judaism and Christianity because of their intolerant claims of exclusivity and historical use of violence, not to mention the primitive and mythical elements of Jewish-Christian theology.

The Population Growth Syndrome!

Humanity also needs to obliterate the religious commandments for people to go forth and multiply.

This abused planet doesn't need more people, and the religious-based obsession that it does is another kind of insanity! Who in their right mind can still believe that the Earth needs more millions of poor and oppressed people—or rich and free people for that matter?

While this belief had some justification in earlier times when the population of the Earth was small, life expectancy was short and dangerous diseases often caused mass extinctions. Now, whether expressed or not, the motivation of some religions for unrestricted fertility among their members is primarily to increase their numbers and their financial and political power because they know that virtually all of their membership comes from members having more children, not by proselytizing among adults.

In the past, the proselytizing success that Christianity has had has invariably been in poor countries where women especially were oppressed. These successes did not come from the theology or spirituality the missionaries preached but from the gender and social reforms they advocated.

The mistreated and unhappy people in these countries should have learned long ago that believing in, bowing before, and praying to spirits and gods did not improve their political or social situation one iota. That was something that required fundamental reforms in political and social institutions over which they had no control whatsoever.

The Mormon religion is one partial exception in the proselytizing gambit to increase its membership. Not-withstanding the infantile fable story of its founding, the Mormon Church follows a system that in many respects is far more practical and positive than that of other religions.

Its emphasis on language and culture learning, on strict dress and behavior and on business acumen has made it a powerful force that is attractive to people who are still struggling to achieve peace-of-mind, security and prosperity.

But the positive side of the Mormon campaign to increase its number of members does not alter the fact that the whole population-growth concept is like a virus that has infected the Big Three religions since their founding.

The religious-economic-political concept that prosperity and the quality of life is based on a continuously growing population is not only outdated, it is one of the primary factors in the poverty that plagues over half of the population of the Earth, including millions of people in the most prosperous nations.

Over-population is also one of the primary sources of much of the violence that afflicts so much of mankind.

The Distant Dream

All of the prevailing reasons why men go to war—religion, the hunger for political power, the obsession with wealth, territorial ambitions, oppressive government regimes—should be eliminated by a coordinated universal effort that now seems to be so far beyond the power of mankind that it is not even a dream.

But that is exactly what at least 95 percent of the people on Earth want! So why can't it be done?

It *can* be done but it will not be done until religious and political leaders are no longer in the dark ages where ignorance, irrationality and inhuman behavior are the norm—the norm for them; not for the people at large—or until new more powerful forces transform the mindset of humanity...a phenomenon that is already underway.

One of the most positive factors that has already raised the living standards of people in China and India—two countries that represent some two-thirds of humanity—is work and production outsourcing from the United States, Japan, South Korea and other developed countries.

As controversial and as painful to some as this phenomenon has been, it nevertheless is the most efficient and practical means of achieving economic parity between nations—not tearing any of them down, but building all of them up.

The more affluent China, India and other developing countries become, the more they contribute to the economy of the countries out-sourcing to them, the more stable their governments, and the more likely the leaders are to cherish and work for peace and prosperity.

Of course, there are many other things that should be done. And despite all of the gloom and doom scenarios I've harped on the great majority of people on this endangered planet are good-hearted, well-behaved and hardworking, and, again, want only to live peaceful, comfortable, secure lives.

The truly evil doers—leaders and their henchmen who are actually well-known to the world—number only in the thousands. If the world could somehow get rid of them and prevent others from taking their place the Earth could and surely would become a sane, safe habitat for humanity in a very short period of time.

It is obvious that the material quality of life is primarily determined by knowing what to do and having the political and religious freedom to do it. This makes it imperative that all people be freed from the destructive religious, political and economic shackles of the past.

The Declining Power of America

With the inevitable ascendancy of China, India and other developing countries the United States will just as inevitably become a second or third-rate world power if American leaders in all fields do not accept the idea that the American cultural paradigm of the 20th century is obsolete, and implement more comprehensive and practical, steps to actually live up to the ideals espoused by virtually everyone in positions of leadership but seldom if ever lived up to by most of them.

This especially applies to the bureaucratic and institutionalized leadership in academia, education and politics, where self-interest rules.

American scientists have made great progress in beginning the process of getting the world's population under control—and this may very well be the one of the most important contributions made to both humanity and the Earth. See *Chapter [19] Saving the Earth & Humanity.*

[2]
Why Males Discriminate
Against Females!

Male discrimination against females did not begin as a religious thing. It evolved naturally from the genetic programming of males, so when men created gods the gods naturally consigned women to an inferior status.

Males in virtually all species are genetically designed to be sexually aggressive, to impregnate as many females as possible and to take by force and keep exclusive sexual rights to as many females as possible.

As noted before, this instinctive behavior was buttressed by the male recognition that *females are inherently more sexually potent than males.*

Females can engage in sex dozens of times a day whether they really want to or not because they don't have to get a hard-on to do it and are not as exhausted as males are by the sexual climax—if they have one.

Males on the other hand, more often than not, achieve sexual climaxes in a matter of minutes because in earlier times engaging in sex left them susceptible to attack by competing males so they had to do it quickly.

Furthermore, most males, including younger ones, cannot repeat the sex act more than two or three times in rapid succession and still enjoy it. It not only loses its power to pleasure, it becomes painful.

And it was this sexual reality that resulted in early males doing everything in their power—physically, emotionally, intellectually and spiritually—to control women, to make them subservient not only sexually but in all other aspects of life.

While some primate species, like monkeys, can perform sexually several times a day day-after-day, even the most potent [young!] human male is satiated after three or four times at most. When a human male achieves a sexual climax it releases the sexual energy that has built up over a period of time, and it takes time for this energy to rebuild.

By the time the average male is in his mid-30s this buildup of sexual energy generally requires two or three if not more days, during which his interest in sex is mental instead of a physical need.

The hype that manufacturers use to sell drugs like Viagra—which artificially create erections of the male organ for an hour or more with the promise that men can have sexual intercourse several times a day day-after-day if so desired—is both misleading and dangerous.

The billion-dollar-a-year success of Viagra naturally inspired copycats—the hype of one of them, called Aspire 36 Plus, described as a fast-acting liquid, says that in addition to improving arousal it "enhances the entire experience from beginning to toe-curling end giving you both uninhibited satisfaction yet you'll still be ready for round two, three or four!!!" The ads go on to say that it keeps on working, again and again, "reducing recovery time for your encore performance!"

Males who have a hard-on for more than a half an hour or so without having a climax quickly discover that it is extremely uncomfortable and sometimes very painful if the sexual stimulation from kissing or other activity that doesn't result in a climax is intense and prolonged. Teenage boys who neck with girls for long periods without going all the way find this out soon enough.

Having a hard-on for several hours—as some of the sex drug makers admit—becomes a medical problem that requires the intervention of a doctor who can administer [as you would expect!] another drug to counteract the sex drug.

In other words, it is not natural or actually possible for human males to become as sexually potent as females because nature was not and still is not that equitable. The make-up of male and female sexuality was designed to ensure that life goes on despite all of the dangers it presented—not to make males and females sexual equals.

Subsequent religious taboos, customs and laws designed to control and limit the sexual behavior of both males and females were to have incredible unintentional results.

Generally, the only people who were exempt from these restrictions—or simply chose to ignore them—were the men in charge. Both lay and religious leaders have historically broken the laws they enacted and required common people to obey.

Of course, the greatest scandal to hit the Catholic Church at the end of the 20th century was the revelation of sexual activity by homosexual and pedophile priests—a practice that had been going on for centuries but was kept quiet by Church leaders as well as condoned by those in these categories who had risen to high positions in the Church.

This ongoing situation did not become publicly known nationally or internationally until the advent of news media that was both irreverent and more driven by readership and profit motives. The first reactions of the Catholic Church on the highest level were disingenuous to say the least, but as more and more incidents were revealed and lawsuits mounted, the Church finally came out clearly, admitting the problem and saying it would take steps to stop it.

Celibacy and the Catholic Church

There is also growing lay and some priestly opposition to the Catholic Church doctrine of requiring priests to remain celibate—in part, no doubt, because of the 20th century sex scandals involving priests.

The idea that abstaining from sexual intercourse with members of the opposite sex results in males and females remaining pure, saintly and god-like, goes back several thousand years. It was not until the 4th century A.D. that it first cropped up in the so-called Western Church. And it was not until the mid-11th century that Pope Gregory VII issued a decree forbidding priests from marrying.

The decree prohibiting priests from marrying or engaged in sex with females was reaffirmed by Popes in the 12th century and again in the 16th century. Despite growing opposition to this ancient practice the decree was again reaffirmed in 2010 by Pope Benedict XVI.

The ancient idea that celibacy contributes to purity in both a physical and divine sense is, of course, absolute nonsense. What it does do is subject the individual to enormous stress that manifests itself in a variety of ways that have long been obvious but have been ignored by the Church hierarchy.

[3]
Why Nature Made Women
Sexually Superior to Men!

If I recall my studies of human biology correctly all human beings begin as females, with some of the embryos later developing into males.

This is the first sign that nature ["God!"] intended for the female sex to be superior to the male sex. In any event, it puts the kibosh on the Christian teaching that God first created a man then took a rib out of the poor fellow and created a woman.

As said, the second nature-made factor that virtually ensures the superiority of the females is the in-disputable sexual superiority of females. As noted, females can engage in sex dozens of times a day if they want to [especially if they are getting paid for it!], while even the most virile male peters out after three or four times at the most and has to wait for hours to days before he is able to produce semen, get it up again, and actually enjoy the act.

Males who attempt to go beyond the natural limit of sexual desire end up with sore penises and a dull, throbbing pain in the gonads and prostate gland that lasts from several hours to a day or more.

And finally, the genetic factor that nails the superiority of the female sex is that when women are free to think and behave in a way that is natural for them they are generally more practical, more logical, more rational, and more humane than males—all factors that are essential parts of the make-up of females because they are responsible for the actual creation and nurturing of human life.

If you make up a list of all of the cruel, destructive, evil, inhumane, savage and stupid things that have happened to human beings—and are, of course, still happening today—at least 99 percent of the people responsible for these things have been and are males.

One of the primary reasons for this male mayhem can be traced to the position taken by the three largest and most powerful religious cults [Judaism, Christianity and Islam], which resulted in males having to repress their natural sexual desires and use up their sexual energy in other ways that were often violent.

This religious belief included the concept that women are inherently inferior, making life even more onerous and destructive for females.

In the U.S. and a few other countries the religious concept of female inferiority lost some ground during the 20th century, but even in these countries women are still regarded as and generally treated as inferior to men.

It seems that in the ancient Asian cultures that gave birth to Buddhism, Shintō and some other religious concepts males were wise enough to partially recognize the vital role that females play in the existence and survival of the human species, and did not totally imprison females in doctrine-based chains.

I submit that humanity will continue to be plagued by ignorance, stupidity and violence as long as religious doctrines continue to preach and enforce the superiority of men and the inferiority of women, and prevent women from bringing their innate sense of compassion, cooperation and goodwill to the world at large.

Obviously, the sexual nature of males and the sex-based arrogance that led them to automatically assume that they were superior to females was to have results that went far beyond the oppression of females.

This arrogance and the cultural systems it created continue to plague mankind, and despite the examples of women who have ascended to power in the business and political worlds the underlying faults and failures of the religious-inspired syndrome remain in control in most societies.

[4]

When Males Get Hard
On the Bottom
They Get Soft on Top!

What nature apparently did not foresee or plan for was the possibility that male members of the human species would not always have ready access to females for sexual purposes. Males were designed with their gonads always in the "on" position, producing semen and sexual energy 24 hours a day.

The problem with this is that when males are prevented—for whatever reason—from expelling all of the sexual energy that builds up in their gonads and prostate glands it spreads throughout their bodies, including their brains.

The pressure from this unused energy builds up and up, and fairly early in the process begins to affect how males think and act. As I have repeated for decades, "when males get hard on the bottom they get soft on the top!"

It is easy—or at least it should be easy—for both males and females to recognize this sexual energy overload because the attitudes and behavior of males change from what might be described as their normal, rational self.

However, the early signs of sex energy overload are subtle. Most males are forced to attempt to keep the signs hidden—or they choose to keep them hidden for a variety of reasons, including both petty and major emotional factors, as well as social and legal restraints.

Males in most cultures have, of course, been programmed to conceal and suppress their sexual desires except in specific and limited situations because the customs and rules of their society determine the sexual behavior that is acceptable or taboo. And, of course, the sexual mores of societies are primarily determined by whatever religious influence has been paramount since ancient times.

So what does the world have as a result of the disparity in male and female sexuality and the religious attempts to keep males on top and females on the bottom? It has an environment in which the primitive instincts of males continue to influence every aspect of human life; and in which many of the elements in human life are irrational, harmful and destructive.

Traditionally, American females have been among those who were deliberately kept ignorant of their own sexual nature as well as that of males. In this day and age it is absolutely incredible to admit that just a few generations ago women were subject to being tied to stakes and burned alive by men who accused them of being witches when they exhibited "unnatural" behavior—generally the result of sex-related frustrations.

It was not until well into the 20th century that a few women began to rebel against the sexual restraints and discrimination females were forced to endure, by writing and speaking and eventually creating a movement that came to be known as "Women's Lib."

The partial success of this movement was a direct outgrowth of the new entertainment and news media industries jumping on the Women's Lib band-wagon—not so much because they had become advocates but because of prurient interest in the stories and the fact that they grabbed attention and increased sales profits.

But Women's Lib has made only a small dent in the behavior of males driven by unused sexual energy and a mindset that is still in an ancient self-interest mode based on physical strength, size and an "in-charge" complex that often ignores reality.

Of course, there are millions of civilized and educated men who have risen above this ancient male programming, and their influence is growing but it is far from the point that it can change the course of the institutions that control the bulk of humanity.

As is so obvious it goes without saying that even the most enlightened societies today remain in the grips of ancient patterns of thought and behavior that are patently irrational and destructive not only to human beings but to the Earth and all of its other life forms.

But it also goes without saying that for the first time in human history the knowledge that is necessary to change this doomsday scenario is at hand and the desire for change is growing. The question is: when will this knowledge really begin to make significant inroads on the power structures that are now in charge?

[5]
The Misuse & Abuse
of
Male Sexuality!

The religious and social taboos against natural male promiscuity and the social customs and laws that have evolved to control the sexual behavior of males since the dawn of civilizations have had incredible results that impact on every aspect of human life—many of them negative.

One of the most incredible of these results is the relationship between violence and unused male sexual energy. Studies by professionals have shown that the more sexual energy that builds up in males the more likely they are to engage in behavior that includes every form of violence known, including extreme physical violence.

As noted earlier, the more buildup of sexual energy in males the less mental control they have and the more likely they are to engage in disruptive and destructive behavior. This behavior ranges from emotional and verbal abuse of children, girl friends and wives to fighting and mass murder.

The results of incarcerating huge numbers of men in prisons where they do not have access to normal sexual release—with females—are well known, but in many countries, including the U.S., religious taboos have traditionally prevented such access, and now the cost of such a system and administrative factors work against it.

Mexico, touted as a Catholic country, allows many of its prison inmates to have conjugal visits from wives and girl friends, particularly those who can afford to pay their jailors a fee for the privilege.

This situation exists in Mexico because like other typical Hispanic-influenced Catholic countries most of the men pay no attention to the dictates of the Church [except perhaps on Sundays and special holidays]—looking at religious beliefs and real life as separate worlds. There is even a special term for this division of real life and religious life in the Philippines.

The Incredible Masturbation Taboos

The role of the Christian Church in attempting to control the sexual behavior of males has included taboos against masturbation. Until recent times the Church taught that achieving sexual release through masturbation was a sin against God. There is scripture in the Bible that says it is better for males to screw whores than cast their seed to the wind.

And until recent times some preachers and priests advised mothers of young boys to tie their hands be-hind their backs at night so they couldn't masturbate while in bed. [It is normal for males to get hard-on's from four to a dozen times every 24 hours, including while asleep...which often wakes them up as they get older.]

As late as the mid-20th century some Christianized mothers were still telling their young sons that masturbating would make them go insane—and those who do it today do so furtively so as not to be caught and shamed by their parents or other adults. Masturbating by girls has been even more taboo.

Thanks to the religious position on masturbation, the urge and need to masturbate has, of course, given rise to a large industry that manufactures and sells dildos and other masturbation tools.

Sex Has Never Been Just about Procreation

It is indisputable that the role that human sexuality plays in so-called developed societies, especially in the U.S., has less to do with procreation than it does with pure pleasure, politics and business across the board, particularly in the so-called entertainment industries, and it is a major factor in all other areas of life as well.

In fact, the irrational aspects of human societies go well beyond the problems of dealing with human sexuality, and can be seen in every area of existence, from parental influence, education, the economy, the political world and, of course, the spiritual world.

Certainly not all cultures that repress human sexuality are pathological in every nook and cranny of their existence, but there are enough pathological elements in all of them that brutality, barbarism, emotional suffering, intellectual dishonesty, spiritual dishonesty and venality are common—and often the rule—in every area of life.

As said, the male reaction to the repression of natural sexual desire is behavior that ranges from unnatural to obsessive and violent. Of course, most males strive to suppress the physical and emotional pressure they experience from sexual energy overload in order to conform to expectations and stay out of trouble.

Some of this energy can be dissipated by strenuous physical and mental activity, and this has been an important factor in the success of many males. But ultimately, one way or another, the unnatural suppression of sexual energy has a deleterious effect on the lives of males, beginning with puberty—and this effect naturally carries over to females, with some of the worst instances involving the rape of females of all ages, from very young children to the elderly.

In the beginning men created God in their own image, thereafter everything went to Hell!

—Boyé Lafayette De Mente—

Another Hard-On Dilemma!

As said, healthy males get a hard-on's from four to eight or more times every 24-hour period, starting when they are still in the womb and continuing until they are in their 70s, 80s or 90s if they live that long.

In advanced countries today men are living into their 70s and 80s and beyond, and during these long life-spans they are having far more erections per day and night than was normal for males in the past be-cause there is more overt sexual stimulation.

This means the average male get from 2,000 to 3,000 hard-on's per year, of which less than 10 percent are used. You can image what kind of physical and emotional stress this causes. No wonder the prostate gland gets enlarged and causes problems in older men!

In addition to this natural phenomena, by the time boys in the United States and some other countries are in their mid-teens they have advanced to necking with girl friends, during which they typically have full, hard, unrelieved erections for as long as an hour or more. This results in significantly increasing the build-up of stress in their prostate glands and gonads—often to the point that it is extremely painful.

Furthermore, the amount of sexual titillation that present-day males of all ages are exposed to for several hours a day on television, in magazines, movies, etc., is incredible, and dramatically in-creases the incidence of regular, daily sexual stress that is not relieved, even by masturbation.

If you assume that a male has a partial or complete erection only five times every 24-hour period and lives to be 60 years old that amounts to a total of 109,500 erections. I am sure you can assume that these erections were not "used" more than about 100 times a year, for a total of 6,000 during the 60-year period. This leaves males with well over 100,000 unrelieved sexual arousals over a period of six decades.

The negative impact this accumulation of stressed-out periods has on the prostate gland has to be horrific—and I believe is the primary cause of enlargement of the prostate gland...and may also be associated with the incidence
of prostate cancer.

For every year beyond 60 that you add to the lifespan of men you have at least an additional 1,800-plus erections—and despite old tales you might have heard, normal, healthy men in their 60s, 70s and 80s *do* get hard-on's, and suffer when they are not used.

It's Not a Laughing Matter!

Those who are tempted to laugh this problem off as some-thing that is not really serious would be well advised to seriously consider that unrelieved sexual stress among males is one of the primary sources of all of the male-generated violence that has plagued mankind from the beginning.

The longer normal, healthy males go without re-leasing the natural buildup of sexual energy the more apt they are to engage in some kind of violence—from abusing their wives and children to taking their frustrations out on other members of society—or engaging in other kinds of destructive behavior.

As I have observed so many times, when a man gets hard on the bottom he gets soft on the top—meaning he cannot think in clear, rational terms and is likely to do irrational things when in a state of sexual arousal.

So, what is the solution to the problem of all of the erections males get and have no opportunity to use? Masturbation is generally effective when early teenage boys are concerned. But masturbation is not the ideal solution for adult men. It relieves the physical stress but not the emotional stress and relief doesn't last long.

[6]
The Misuse & Abuse
of
Female Sexuality!

Until recent times virtually all societies ignored the fact that women also have powerful sexual urges and needs—an incredible arrogance perpetrated by males. The emotional and physical suffering this has caused and continues to cause females is incal-culable.

It seems that only a few Pacific island societies ever developed practices that came close to solving this problem for both males and females—customs that Christian missionaries quickly banned as soon as they gained control of the lives of the islanders.

Polynesian sexual customs included older women initiating young boys, and older men initiating young girls into sexual activities.

For more details about the erotic lives of Polynesians see my book, *ROMANTIC HAWAII – Sun, Sand, Surf and Sex.*

Over the millennia the various ailments females suffered from being denied the opportunity to fulfill their sexual needs were invariably linked by males to the overall nature of females—not sexual deprivation. Some men, however, consciously or subconsciously, apparently realized that there was a sexual element in the "disruptive" behavior of females, and their often stated solution was that they needed a "good screw."

However, this insight did not lead to any lessening of the male-created taboos that kept females from being able to use up their sexual energy.

Some of the measures promoted or condoned by the Christian Church during the so-called Middle Ages to control female sexual behavior are hardly believable today.

Beginning in the 11th century, European church and lay leaders launched a series of religious-inspired military campaigns against Middle East countries in an attempt to free Jerusalem and the other "Holy Cities" from their Moslem occupiers.

These so-called "Crusades" against Islamic countries continued off and on for approximately three hundred years.

During this incredibly long period of Pope-backed wars some men had their wives outfitted with "chastity belts"—iron thong-like devices that were locked in place to prevent the women from being able to have sexual intercourse with other males while the husbands were away doing their religious duty.

Many of these lockable iron "chastity belts" were made in Italy, where their manufacture and use was promoted by the Catholic Church. [Even farther out than this device was an older practice among ancient slave holders to have the foreskin of the penises of their adult male slaves sewn tight, leaving only a tiny hole for urination, to discourage them from engaging in sexual intercourse with any woman; another extreme to which men have gone in the past to control sexual behavior.]

Ironically, most of the glory-hungry knights who left Europe in their zeal to take the "Holy Land" away from Moslems never returned home. Some 20 percent of them were killed in battle, and some 60 or 70 percent of them died from the plague and other diseases. History also notes, not surprisingly, that many women managed to get around the iron chastity belts by one means or another, including having a second key made by willing locksmiths.

Despite all of the advances
in knowledge
in all areas of human life
the evolution of human
males has not yet caught up
with the times.
As a result females are
gradually taking over—
something I have been
predicting and advocating
for decades.

—Boyè Lafayette De Mente—

According to a number of totally unreliable sources on the Internet some form of chastity belts continued to be used in Europe well after the end of the Crusades, and, in fact, into modern times. Such is the terrible hold that religious beliefs have on both men and women.

In more recent times, males have primarily relied on religious teachings, laws and social sanctions to keep women from expending their unused sex energy...and this is still the prevailing situation in most societies today. But the day of women is coming.

[7]
The Use of Sexual
Titillation in Business!

One of the most incredible results of the misunderstanding, misuse and abuse of human sexuality in the so-called Western world [which equates with the Christianized nations] has been the dramatic appearance and growth of sexual titillation industries since the advent of movies and television in the early 1900s.

This doesn't mean there was no sex-oriented media in earlier times. Drawings, paintings and even sculptures have long depicted men and women in the nude and in sex acts for their arousal effects.

In fact, in earlier times cultures in some Asian countries had enormous industries devoted to such things. Early Japan's famous 69-position sex charts are now collector's items worth large sums of money, and its annual sex festivals continue to attract hundreds of thousands of viewers. Sex-oriented sculptures of India, Cambodia and other Southeast Asian countries also continue to attract large numbers of tourists.

Sex-oriented novels—most of them aimed at fe-males—began to sell by the millions in the early 1900s. By the mid-1900s printed "fuck" comics and cartoons were big things in American high schools, furtively passed around by giggling girls and smirking boys in the classrooms and hall-ways. [Popeye was a popular star in the cartoons!]

But it was not until the hippie movement in the late 1950s and 1960s had influenced and liberated movie and television producers and magazine publishers that sexual titillation became one of the biggest in-dustries in the country and one of the foundations of the whole economy.

As early as the 1970s hardcore porn films were available on television in hotel rooms, and despite some half-hearted attempts to stop the practice it continues—protected by the Freedom of Speech amendment attached to the American Constitution.

Visual and verbal pornography are now a mainstay of the movie and television industries. Even the broadcast news media has joined the sexual titil-lation crowd by selecting sexy female newscasters who are groomed fit to kill, wear short skirts, reveal a lot of naked leg and flirt with both guests and viewers.

As of this writing films showing both partial and complete nudity are now common fare on some television channels. Sexual intercourse showing [depicting] everything except the entry of the male penis into the female vagina is common.

In the 1970s I predicted that hardcore porn would soon be available on television for a fee at the push of a button. That had happened by the 1980s, and now on some channels it is free because sponsors are willing to pay for it. Some hardcore porn programs have millions of viewers daily.

[8]
Why Sex is Used to Sell Everything!

Another of the incredible and conspicuous aspects of the failure of males in Jewish, Christian and Islamic societies to understand and deal humanely and effectively with the sexual nature of men and women is the fact that the display of female sexuality has become the foundation of marketing in the United States, with several European and Hispanic countries following suit. [The sexual nature of some Mexican family TV fare, in advertising and entertainment, is really something.]

By 2005 even once sex-staid China has boarded the sex-marketing bandwagon, and it will be very interesting to watch this development, both because the Chinese have a different cultural background regarding sex and because of the conservative influence that the Communist Party still has on the country.

The fact that it is primarily the use of *female* sexuality that primes the business pump in America and other Christianized countries is yet other outcome of the Jewish and Christian religions historically keeping women in the shadows and subservient to men—denying them the right of self-expression and making the subject of their sexuality both taboo and a subject of obsessive interest among males.

Islam has been and still is even more rigid and extreme in its efforts to keep women in serfdom—a primitive practice that goes all the way back to caveman days and is just now beginning to show cracks because a tiny percentage of Islamic women have become educated enough, affluent enough and courageous to loosen the religious chains that have bound them since ancient times.

Hopefully, the influence of international television will eventually override the hold that Islamic law has on females, allowing them to become fully realized human beings.

Another of the results of the religious-inspired laws requiring women to keep their bodies covered is that males in these countries have developed a fetish about female breasts. Surely never in the history of mankind has more been made about any part of the human body than what is now seen in the U.S., Mexico and other countries in regards to female tits.

Your might think that an American mother being arrested for breastfeeding her baby in public has to be the epitome of stupidity. But then along comes an Islamic cleric who announces in the Iranian media that women who engage in promiscuous behavior and whose dress reveals breast cleavage and leg not only corrupts young men and leads to adultery but is also the cause of earthquakes.

This example of religious idiocy prompted Purdue University genetics and evolution student Jennifer McCreight to create a 'boobquake" Facebook group as a joke…"to help fight supernatural thinking and the oppression of women just because they showed some cleavage."

In a matter of hours over 105,000 female *Facebook* users had volunteered to join the group, resulting in news media around the world picking up on the story. The site will probably become big and profitable—with many newcomers logging on because they think it is as online pornography and they are going to see a lot of boobs.

What a marvelous story and what an amazing example of the power of the Internet to reveal the ongoing idiocy and stupidity of primitive religious thinking and the susceptibility of the human mind to being programmed to believe anything.

Bras especially designed to reveal a lot of tit are big sellers. Plastic surgeons [mostly males] reacting to demand from hundreds of thousands of women have turned enlarging tits into another new industry.

But given the direction and the speed with which the breast fetish is driving "fashion" it seems safe to predict that totally bare breasts will eventually become so commonplace in public that the fetish will peter out.

Genuine ignorance is profitable
because it is likely to be accompanied by humility, curiosity and open mindedness,
whereas ability to repeat catch-phrases, cant terms and familiar propositions gives the
conceit of learning and coats the mind with varnish [that is] waterproof [immune] to new ideas.

—John Dewey—

So What's Next, the Male Penis?

Will the size and appearance of the erect male organ ever become a fetish among liberated females? I predicted that it would in *EROS' REVENGE – Brave New World of American Sex,* [written in the 1960s], and when it happens it will result in nationally televised contests and awards—resulting in fame and wealth for the extra-endowed men. [Basketball players would have to be banned from entering these contests because they would win most of them.]

Interestingly, centuries before Christianity became the primary religion in Rome sports-minded Romans staged penis contests in the gladiator stadium. The description of these popular coed events that especially caught my attention was the one about a man whose erect penis was so long he rested it on a wheel barrier as he proudly paraded it around the arena to rousing applause from the audience.

Such an event today would surely outdraw golf, and sponsors would be lined up by the hundreds.

The use of female sexuality to market products will no doubt continue until the sexuality of women is out in the open and no longer of obsessive interest to either males or females. That could be a long time coming because the influence of religions will remain strong for the foreseeable future.

[9]
The Profit Motive
As the New Morality!

Industrialization has resulted in the decline of religions as the foundation of human morality. The Catholic Church in particular has become a huge commercial and political enterprise, more concerned with profit and growth—and keeping males on top—than with the spiritual lives of its members.

In fact, the Catholic Church has been more interested in profits and politics than in truth and in the quality of life since before the Middle Ages, but it was only with the dramatic increase in knowledge and the educational level of the laity that it began to lose spiritual relevance. The Pope and his huge staff of generals have become business managers, more interested in profit-and-loss than in convincing members that they will go to Heaven when they die if they follow the ancient dictates of the Church.

The loss of religion-based morality in business, politics and society in general—as inhuman and as discriminatory as it always has been—was nevertheless a real loss because it at least had some standards of conduct for people in charge that sometimes benefitted those without power.

Now, there is no area of human endeavor that is not controlled by the profit motive, and more often than not profit takes precedence over any abstract religious morality that has survived. This includes education and politics in addition to every category of business.

Well before the turn of the 21st century the rise of the profit morality had become even more complicated because of the increasing international demand for oil and raw materials to feed the insatiable maws of modern life.

The Foreign Affairs Dilemma

As is well known, all industrially advanced countries that do not have sufficient oil, iron ore, copper and a various other raw materials now compete with each other politically as well as economically.

This has resulted in a situation in which profit-oriented have-nots are essentially hostages to the haves, creating a foreign affairs dilemma for many nations, especially the U.S., for which there are no fast, easy solutions.

War, which has traditionally been the solution to such problems, is no longer an easy option. Having to deal with rogue, unfriendly nations that are major suppliers of oil or other critical resources makes the problems even more complicated.

Contemplating what this could mean for mankind on a short-term is not a pleasant experience. But the bright side of this dilemma is that it is forcing leaders to talk instead of fight, and is encouraging them to do the things they should have been doing anyway at least for decades if not centuries—and that, of course, is developing new benign sources of energy, creating new green products and developing a green lifestyle.

The optimistic view is that there is enough innate goodness in most of humanity that when the huge mass of ordinary people reach the mindset that things must change, and achieve the ability to force these changes on those in power, a universal moral-ity that is rational, logical, practical and beneficial will emerge.

There are going to be many dark decades before that happens, but there is hope. In addition to wind and solar power there is also the probability that oil produced from algae and other green sources could supplement power needs until efforts to harness energy from nuclear fusion becomes a reality.

When oil is replaced by other energy sources, the changes that will occur in politics and economics could be as fundamental as discovering how to make and control fire.

In an odd twist of fate, the only profit-making competitor that is even more powerful than oil is pornography. It is easy and cheap to produce, and can be distributed around the world in one second, at virtually no cost.

Porn Has Become the "Mother Load!"

When early gold and silver miners discovered the main vein of these valuable metals they referred to it as striking "the Mother Load."

By the turn of the 21st century the richest Mother Load in history was not gold or silver. It was pornography. Today, some of the richest people in the world are pornographers who no longer have to depend on printed magazines, movies and sleazy theaters to peddle their products.

The advent of television and the Internet provided pornographers with the means to reach hundreds of millions of customers in a matter of minutes, at little or virtually no production cost.

As incredible as it seems on the surface, the right to produce, distribute and sell pornography is protected by the "Freedom of Speech" provision in the American Bill of Rights...a right repeatedly reaffirmed by the Supreme Court of the United States and buttressed by an army of lawyers paid by pornographers.*

---

*In the 1970s *Hustler* magazine publisher Larry Flynt had a attorney on a $15,000 a month retainer to fight off lawsuits if and when they occurred. This monthly expense was probably next only to the cost of printing the magazine but it was pocket change to the publisher. Despite the unsavory media-created reputation Flynt had as a smut peddler, he had goals that were more admirable than those claimed by many religions. His aim was to force people to be honest and aboveboard about their prejudices and obsessions, face them, and overcome them. He knew his approach was shocking to the average person. He also knew absolutely that it would make him immensely rich. But he was honest about it. I was in Larry's tiny apartment sharing a fold-over peanut butter sandwich with him when a courier from a bank delivered a certified one million dollar check to him.

A year or so later I was sharing a luxurious Las Vegas apartment with Larry when he said to me: "Boye, you taught me everything I know about publishing. How come I'm rich and you're not?"

I didn't have to grope for an answer. "Because your balls are bigger than mine" I replied.

The incredible market for porn was not created by the pornographers. It was created by the religious teachings that sexual behavior outside of marriage and for the purpose of procreation was a sin against a vengeful god and those guilty of ignoring these teachings would go to Hell.

To prevent men from being aroused and seduced by females the religions mandated that women keep their bodies covered and not engage in any kind of licentious behavior. The sanctions against these mandates included death—a pathological male-leader response that is still in force in present-day Islam.

The very successful efforts of religions to deny, ignore and subvert both male and female sexuality naturally resulted in males becoming pathologically obsessive about female sexuality.

Male pornographers are not the only ones who take advantage of this cultural aberration. Since women are naturally smarter than men, some of them have also taken advantage of the male obsession with female sexuality to create their own porn sites; and, of course, both businessmen and entertainers use female sexuality as one of the primary elements in selling their products.

Sex is never going to lose its appeal and power be-cause it is built into the human genes but it is becom-

ing so common that it will eventually not be controversial on controlled by laws.

Butts and Breasts!

Interestingly, promoting prurient interest in female
breasts had gone so far by the turn of the century that
marketers in the fashion industry had begun to zero
in on female butts as the new thing. Some of the
television commercials focusing on the butts of
shapely females are more sexually arousing than the
cleavage and tit ads because female butts are far
more directly associated with actual sexual intercourse than breasts.

Pornographers of whatever stripe should bow down
daily to the anti-human sex-distorting religious leaders for creating the "mother load" they mine so
profitably.

There is no question
that religious-based morality
has failed mankind…
because males are still
in charge!
—*Boyè Lafayette De Mente*—

[10]
The Incredible American
Gulag System!

One of the most conspicuous examples of the ills of American society today is the number of people [mostly males] in prison. I believe that on a per capita basis the United States has more people in prison than any other country in the world. Given our history and our self image that is an absolutely astounding and shocking statistic.

There have to be reasons for this unbelievable fact, and these reasons go to the very heart of contemporary American culture. The reality is that we do not have a single coherent, cohesive culture that is both positive and progressive. We have a mishmash of cultures that are a combination of the worst and the best in human nature, and at this time the worst is on top.

The huge chain of gulag prisons in the country is just one symptom of the failures that are found in every part of society, from the family environment and child-raising to education, business, the so-called entertainment industries, to the legal system and politics.

And, of course, it is a given that the large religious organizations in the country are virtually impotent in the face of brainwashing made possible by new technology, and are no longer the primary sources of morality—as skewered as it always has been.

The morality of American society is now in the hands of a babble of money-driven entertainment moguls, drug dealers and a coterie of elected politicians in a money-driven system of government that controls the law enforcement agencies and lawyer-trained judges—a system that is not only stupid, it guarantees moral de-gradation and disaster.

The United States became a world power not because of its Constitution and Bill of Rights and its democratic ideals and institutions, but because of a series of serendipitous circumstances that began with stealing the huge country from its first in-habitants—killing most of them in the process—having access to enormous resources that were free for the taking; and allowing freewheeling entrepreneurs to build empires on the backs of poor people mostly comprised of recent immigrants and slaves.

Of course there were astounding benefits to the democratic ideals that left people free to start businesses, innovate and create a large affluent middleclass and a rich upper class. There were wide swathes of rot in this system but the country was so big and had become so industrially powerful be-cause of wars in Europe and elsewhere that these failings were easily ignored until the first years following the end of World War II in 1945.

But by the end of the 1950s this anything goes attitude had allowed the rot to get out of hand and spread into the family environment and the educa-tion system, destroying much of the role these institutions had traditionally played in American life.

By the end of the 1960s hordes of university students were descending upon beach resorts in the U.S., Mexico and elsewhere during Spring Break, egged on by the resort marketers to leave their inhibitions and morals at home. This led to hundreds of thousands of coeds in skimpy bikinis conger-gating on the beaches and filling the dance clubs at night. Some of them also began exposing their breasts at public events. Others began appearing on balconies completely nude to the raucous shouts of encourage-ment from horny male students. One can certainly assume that this annual event is not limited to flashing tits and standing nude on a balcony.

This change in the religious-based morality of American life has now gone beyond the tipping point and is evolving at a faster and faster speed—without rational, humane guidelines.

Self interest and corporate interest are now the tails wagging the dogs, particularly in government, in the financial industry, and in the food and drug industries. The biggest drug lords in the world are not in Mexico or Columbia. They are in corporate America. The government itself has been mainlining on drug money from alcohol and tobacco since the early days.

The half-witted attempts to deal with this morass of immorality and conflicting interests are feeding the prison population in the U.S., making the gulag system of prisons one of the fastest growing Indus-tries in the country.

Solving these problems will require the creation and implementation of a new, universal culture that is nowhere in sight. But there are encouraging examples in Europe, where some of the prison systems are both humane and actually aimed at rehabilitating inmates.

[11]
How American Males
Are Becoming "Girly Men!"

Actor/governor Arnold Schwarzenegger coined a telling phrase when he described some of his political opponents as "girly men." But this suggestive phrase is equally applicable to a growing percentage of all American men.

In fact, the prevailing culture in America is rapidly making the ancient stud image and behavior of men obsolete—and what it is doing to American women is even more thought provoking. While American boys are being programmed to be girly men, American girls are being brain-washed to be stud women.

This remarkable situation is not something that began in recent times. Much of it can be attributed to the Industrial Revolution which started in England in the late 1700s. This revolution changed the way most men work, and was to have a number of effects that were surely never imagined during its first two hundred years.

For one thing, historical records note that in the early years of America most men in rural areas could lift up to four hundred pounds or more, even though they were smaller in body-build than present-day males.

The typical man today would strain a gut trying to lift half that amount.

Brilliance is typically the act of an individual, but incredible stupidity can usually be traced to an organization.

—Jon Bentley—

Machines Have Replaced Muscles

One of the most important of the effects of Industrialization—the use of machines instead of male muscle—was the gradual reduction in the need for men to be burly, brave and he-men (sexually speaking) to attract women. Another effect of the revolution was that during World War II it resulted in large numbers of women becoming part-time homemakers and full-time factory workers.

This fundamental cultural shift in male and female behavior slowly but surely changed the nature of male and female relations. Among other things, the con-version to a money economy had a profound impact on the way men and women saw each other.

In fact, being a success in business and having money (no matter how it was obtained) was often more effective in attracting playmates and mates than muscles and a strong sex drive. Many women were obviously more turned on by thoughts of wealth than by fantasizing about actual bedroom encounters with men.

By the 1920s the basic image that upper middle class and top class American women had of men had gone so far in reverse from the old caveman figure that there was no comparison. They were attracted to men who never smelled of sweat, were classy dressers, always neat in their appearance, and had good table manners.

Then along came movies and such novels as *The Great Gatsby* by F. Scott Fitzgerald, which glorified the lifestyle of "girly men"—the phrase former terminator-actor Arnold Schwarzenegger called politicians who behaved as if they did not have *cojones* (which is Mexican for balls!).

The "Buffooning" of American Males

By the 1950s the movies, novels and comic strips often ganged up on the masculine take-charge type of male, and made men buffoons who not only couldn't keep a stiff upper lip in emotional situations, there were other things they couldn't keep up as well. One the most famous of the de-neutered males in American history is Dagwood in the *Blondie* comic strip. There is never any doubt about who wears the pants in the Bumsted family. The fact that the strip has survived since the 1930s and is still going strong and evolving says a lot about American culture. Today's Blondie, the wife, has led and kept up with the times by becoming much more "man-like" in her behavior.

The Homosexual Factor

It has long been suspected by some people that "anti-masculine men" movies proliferated because so many of the movie producers and stars were homosexuals who brought their feminine-oriented mindset to their image of the ideal male.

Then the Women's Lib movement took over with a number of powerful books leading the charge, claiming that women should be treated exactly like men, with all of the standard male rights and special privileges.

Many of the claims and charges made by these feminist writers were, in fact, valid, and could not be denied or ignored by the male bastion. Very slowly but surely the male-dominated business establishment began to shed some of its exclusively masculine policies and practices and catering in various degrees to female employees.

This was good, but the most powerful and strident voices among the feminist battalions were not satisfied with just gaining equal rights with men. They were determined to eradicate the traditional masculine male mindset altogether.

The campaigns of the feminist forces were supported and magnified by the mass media that sees anything controversial as fodder for its insatiable profit-driven appetite.

Large numbers of journalists and commentators took up the feminist message, calling on all women to take up arms and assert themselves emotionally, economically and sexually—something they have done with glee and great success.

No More Feminine Mystery

One of the most powerful elements of the feminist message was that women should throw off all of the ancient religious-oriented sexual restraints and taboos, and both glory in and flaunt their sex. This alone has now gone so far that in the United States there is no longer any mystery about the feminine body and feminine sexuality. It is exposed and paraded before the public 24 hours a day.

The message of the extreme feminists included the idea that girls and women not only should take the initiative in their sexual behavior, but that it was right and natural for them to be the aggressors since they were far more sexually potent than males. The prurient news media often backed this point up by noting that women could engage in sex with dozens of partners every day, while even the most libido-driven men were pooped after they had climaxed four or five times.

These messages by the feminists and their news media lackeys had a powerful impact on males because men knew only too well that when it came to sexual stamina they were powder puffs in comparison with women—a disturbing knowledge that was no doubt a primary factor in the attempts by primitive as well as modern men to control the sexual behavior of females.

By the end of the 20th century the divorce rate in the United States was around 60 percent, and more and more young women were foregoing marriage altogether in favor of a lifestyle that allowed them to work and to have sexual encounters whenever and with whomever they chose—something that had previously been a prerogative only for some males.

All of these influences combined resulted in an astounding speed-up of the evolutionary process that resulted in males beginning to act more like females in direct proportion to the degree in which females act like males.

As in other species, it seems that nature does not like and will not abide for long two genders that are basically even in their sex drives. Where humanity is concerned, it seems to be nothing more complicated than the fact that the more masculine women behave the more feminine men behave.

Number of Girly Men Growing

Evidence of the growing femininity of American males is so glaringly obvious it doesn't take a Ph.D. to see it. And now, instead of individual feminists leading the charge against masculine men, the entertainment industry and the business industry have taken over the lead.

Boys and men are being incessantly programmed to use deodorants and perfumes of one kind or another. They are being conditioned to have their nails done and their hair styled and to wear earrings. They are being taught to be more sensitive, like women. They are being brain-washed to show off their butts (although this part of the male anatomy may be less attractive to females than to some males).

The trend for women to become the dominate sex is not limited to the United States. It is particularly conspicuous in Japan which does not have as far to go as the U.S. because traditional Japanese culture feminized males to a remarkable degree.

Growing crowds of Japanese men now regularly patronize beauty parlors for the same service that women get, and with the huge cosmetic companies hyping the custom with seductive advertising it will no doubt continue to grow until it becomes the norm.

But in Japan there is a countervailing movement that will probably delay this process well beyond what would otherwise be the case. For centuries Japanese men have typically had small bodies and physiques that in Western terms were more feminine than masculine.

When the Japanese began to encounter large-bodied Westerners and to compete with them for women and other things they felt this physical disparity strongly.

Bodybuilding was first introduced into Japan back in the 1960s but only a very few men were interested. As competition with foreigners increased and the influence of Western movies, television and magazines became stronger, the popularity of bodybuilding began to grow—and the diet changed. Now it is common to see young Japanese men, especially athletes, who are tall and have muscular physiques.

The entertainment industry remains one of the most powerful worldwide influences in programming boys to think and behave like girls. Many of the most popular male singers are more feminine than masculine in their voice, behavior and dress. The constant exposure of young boys to this kind of influence is obvious.

A large percentage of the most popular television shows have more "feminine male" characters than masculine men—and this is not counting the growing number of homosexual characters—real and pretend—that are featured on these shows.

There is, of course, evidence that the percentage of homosexuals in all of the entertainment industries is disproportionately high because of their creative abilities, so the fact that so many television shows portray males exhibiting female behavior should not surprise anyone.

The influence of homosexual themes in movies is, of course, another of the most conspicuous examples of the fundamental shift in the way males are viewed and the kind of male behavior that is ostensibly approved by a big segment of the population.*

---

*Moguls in the entertainment industry and their supporters in the academic world who say that young children are not influenced by the video games they play and what they watch on television and in theaters are, of course, totally wrong.

74

But they get by with this preposterous position because the rest of the country does not have the will to stop them—and with the incredible amounts of money they rake in they can defend themselves when there is any movement to change their ways.

And as long as these businesses can interpret the "Freedom of Speech" Amendment of the Constitution the way they want to this situation will not change.

I think computer viruses should count as life.
I think it says something about human nature
that the only form of life
we have created so far
is purely destructive.
We've created life in
our own image.

—*Stephen Hawking*—

Why the Male Prostate Gland Gets Big!
And this is bringing us closer to what I believe is probably the direct cause of enlarged prostates and urination problems that plague so many men after they reach the age of 60 or so—a point mentioned earlier.

In the case of human beings, the sexual nature of people is exhibited before they are born—at least before male babies are born. Scanning devices clearly show that male babies frequently have penile erections when they are still in the womb. After male babies are born the frequency of erections gradually increases as they mature.

Rough calculation indicates that after birth the typical male has a complete or partial erection anywhere from four to eight times every 24 hours, with many of these occurring during sleep.

Every time an erection occurs a certain amount of stress is put on the prostate gland and the gonads. The longer the erection lasts the stronger the buildup of stress. This stress buildup is a kind of energy that impacts negatively on both the body and mind of the male.

Because of the sexual energy that builds up during erections most boys learn that the pressure can be relieved by masturbating, and soon after they reach puberty, if not before, most masturbate regularly. But they cannot masturbate every time they have an erection because there are rules against doing it in public (so to speak).

Apparently the primary reason why there is very little if any literature on the incidence of prostate and urination problems in pre-modern times is that most men did not live long enough for such problems to develop. Until the 20th century the average lifespan of males even in industrialized countries was below 50.

One aspect of the problem of sex-deprived males and the incredible amount of violence in the country in the United States is the prison system. With over one million men in American prisons the potential for sex-stress related violence is extreme.

As also mentioned, some countries allow men in prison to have conjugal visits from their wives and girls friends…a special privilege they may have to pay for, but at least that is better than the American way.

[12]
How American Females
Are Becoming
More like Males!

It is common knowledge [not accepted by every-body] that males and females have a number of genetic traits that make them think and behave differently.

While the strength of these genetic attributes varies in individuals—sometimes to such a degree that neither the male nor the female concerned behaves within the range that is typical and expected of their gender—the two sexes are usually different enough that they have traditionally thought and lived in two different worlds.

From the beginning of human history there was both figuratively and literally a man's world and a woman's world, and in most societies these two worlds were separated by barriers that were natural as well as those that were created by men to control women.

This latter factor—the creation of artificial barriers by men to control women—apparently came about for the simple reason that human males, like their lower-order animals relatives, were driven by instinct to control the females in their group so they would have guaranteed exclusive sexual access to them.

At first this male rationale was no doubt an individual thing. But as time passed and spirits and gods were created by men they made their dominance over women a divine, spiritual thing mandated by their godly creations—so they could attribute their superiority to the divinities and not have to take any guff from females.

Of course, there have been a number of early societies that were ruled over by women but these women did not become rulers as a result of their own abilities or actions. They invariably inherited their exalted positions because they were members of a powerful ruling family that failed to produce a male heir.

In short, the obvious animal origins of the human race resulted in females automatically being treated as inferior by larger, stronger males, and then when males got around to creating gods they made sure that their gods "created women" as an after-thought to serve men sexually and otherwise.

This situation existed virtually unchanged until recent times—and still today exists to varying degrees in a number of societies, with the largest and most obvious of these being Islamic and Christian. Both Christianity and Islam have traditionally based one of the rationales for their existence on keeping women in their place—meaning uneducated and subservient to men.

Most of the first European colonists who came to America had, of course, been programmed in the rigid, anti-feminine and inhumane sexual taboos that prevailed in England and elsewhere in Europe at that time.

These religious-oriented concepts continued to make a travesty of the sexual lives of both men and women—but especially women—throughout the early history of the United States. The same outmoded concepts of the proper role of women in all areas of life continued to prevail until the mid-1900s.

It may seem unimaginable now but American men who had long regarded themselves as the most enlightened people on the planet did not permit women to vote until well into the 20th century. And still today there are many areas of life in the United States that are either totally forbidden to women, or they are discouraged from attempting to enter these areas.

But this long practice of holding women down and denying them the chance to develop their potential, sexually and otherwise, has now had astounding and unanticipated consequences.

Beginning in the last half of the 19th century a few women began to poke tiny holes in the barriers that men had erected against the entire female race to keep them in their place.

As the years passed, these holes gradually grew bigger and bigger as more and more women joined this earliest group of female pioneers who were determined to break down the male-made barriers that had penned them in and down since the dawn of human history.

How Wars Changed the Female Role

Finally, in the 1920s—after the upheaval of World War I had resulted in hundreds of thou-sands of women joining the workforce and doing jobs previously done only by men—the female revolution in the United States began in earnest. Large numbers of women began to frequent speakeasy nightclubs, to drink and dance with what for the times was wild abandon.

In the 1920s a short-lived but spectacular economic boom spurred the appearance of hundreds of thou-sands of cars that contributed to women having both more frequent and more intimate relations with men as well as providing upper middleclass and upper class women with more independence than females had ever had before.

The advent of movies in the 1920s was soon to be a boon to the growing freedom of females in the United States, dramatically advancing the cause of women.

This incipient female revolution was considerably muted by the depression of the 1930s but the entry of the United States into World War II in 1941 put it back on track—and it has been racing forward at full speed ever since.

Once again millions of American women entered the wartime workforce, and by the end of the war the economy of the country had grown so large with so many new "female-type" occupations that most of these millions never left the workforce when the war ended.

The war took millions of young men away from home and resulted in so many women working out of the home that it changed the traditional family lifestyle and child-raising in fundamental ways.

Women of all ages, including teenage girls, had a degree of personal freedom unprecedented in history—and once they had it there was no way they were going to let it go.

Girls and young women by the millions began to do the things that in the past only boys and men had done. Ordinary girls and women became more fashion conscious. They began to dress and to wear makeup de-signed to attract the attention of males. They became both more aggressive and more recep-tive in their relations with men.

The rapid increase in the number of motion pictures depicting the glamour and sex-filled lives of movie stars became a major influence on the attitudes and behavior of young females.

The widespread proliferation of television from the mid-1950s added to the economic and social revolution that was remaking the mindset of Amer-ican females.

Girls and women began to compete with males in school, in the workplace and in all forms of recreation. In this new environment, the idea that sexual passivity was the natural lot of females began to fade—something that many young men applauded but they had no inkling about where this fundamental change in male-female relations could lead.

Smashing of Sexual Restraints

The 1960s saw the blooming of the hippie movement—a new kind of social protest created by young student-age people in California who were outraged by the faults they saw in the prevailing culture, including the war in Vietnam.

A big part of this movement was doing away with virtually all sexual restraints—a movement that resulted in many young women being able to explore and exercise their sexuality in ways that had not been available to females before. Smoking marijuana became a mainstay of this new culture, and has since spread far and wide, creating a huge industry and powerful drug lords with their own armies.

From that period on the female revolution in the U.S., promoted by movies, television, magazines and feminist books, became an overwhelming force that could not be slowed down, much less stopped.

However, most of the impetus and power that the revolution gained was not specifically related to the aspirations of feminists or the self-motivated expressions of female frustration. Much of the power of the movement came from the built-in male lust for profits that fueled the American economy.

In short, publishers of magazines and books and producers of movies and television shows discovered that sex sells—and the one area of human sexuality that had never been really talked about, much less economically exploited was female sexuality.

By the 1970s the whole entertainment industry was into selling soft-core pornography. By the 1990s soft and hard-core pornography based on female sexuality was one of the largest and most profitable industries in the United States.

In fact, it can be said that by the last decades of the 20th century virtually the entire American economy rested on sexual titillation—ostensibly aimed at men but also appealing to young females. Today, probably as much as 75 percent of all advertising and marketing programs in the United States are based on exploiting the sexual appeal of women.

Teenage girls and young women in various stages of nudity make up a big percentage of all television fare. Most male as well as female pop singers are backed up by teams of semi-nude girls and women who hump and pump and gyrate in simulated sex orgies.

Destruction of the Female Mystique
This so-called entertainment has destroyed most of the mystery, most of the mystique, of feminine sexuality—ripping it away like the proverbial fiction-novel bodice. The subtlety that is a major part of male-female romance has also been drama-tically diminished.

All of the positive attributes that have traditionally distinguished women—their mystery, their subtlety, that indescribable essence of femininity that made them so special—not to mention their importance and prowess in nurturing—have been diminished, more by the actions of money-addicted men than by the legitimate aspirations of women themselves.

Women are now far more sexually exposed and exploited than men, thanks to the overreaction that has resulted from religious-oriented attempts to conceal and control the sexuality of women.

The sexual restraints and taboos that misguided religious leaders placed on women in the early history of civilization condemned them to suffer the punishment of the damned—and still today makes the world of many women a Hell on earth.

The rapidly growing sexual emancipation of American women is both good and bad. The good part is obvious. The bad part is that it is diminishing the fundamental feminine factor in their character and personality, and turning them into quasi-males.

There are now female boxers, female wrestlers, female weight-lifters, female body-builders (some with muscles that are grotesque), females who play football on mostly male teams…and female soldiers who are actually called upon to fight and kill.

The more masculine females become in their behavior, the more nature compensates by making the behavior of men more feminine. And vice-versa: the more feminine the attitudes and behavior of men, the more masculine females become in their thinking and behavior.

So as incredible as it is, men themselves have set the stage for American women to become more masculine—a phenomenon that has already changed the dynamics of male-female relations in the U.S. and will go much further before it reaches some kind of equilibrium…which could be that women will be on top permanently.

Females are, after all, the most sexually potent of the human species—a fact that men have feared and fought against since before our ancestors climbed down out of the trees.

There is extraordinary irony in the fact that the few powerful men who have ruled the Christian churches and Islamic mosques since the inception of these cults have unwittingly played the role of Eros, and particularly in the United States and other so-called Christian societies the former God of Love is now having his revenge.

The day will also come, inevitably, when the Islamic clergy loses its inhuman control over Moslem women and they too will finally be able to express themselves in normal ways.

A New Race of Amazons

Many American women are now taller, heavier and physically stronger than their ancestors. There are female boxers and female wrestlers, and women who play football on mostly male teams. There are women who are into bodybuilding and have muscles that put most men to shame. There are female weightlifters, and women who participate in such things as Alaska's annual 1,150-mile Iditarod dogsled race. [In a race some time ago a woman beat out all of her male competitors, winning the famous event in record time.]

There are women who have sailed solo in small boats across the Atlantic Ocean, women who have swum the English Channel and others who have climbed the tallest mountains on the planet—all things that were once considered the exclusive preserve of men.

These are all things that traditionally have been associated with testosterone—the male hormone. Whether the physical feats performed by present-day women mean that their bodies are now producing testosterone is an interesting piece of speculation if nothing else.

There is no doubt that the level of testosterone in males in general is lower now than what it was in earlier generations, which may be the result of two factors: women are now competing with men in testosterone-type activities resulting in men producing less of the male sex hormone, and the activities of most present-day men do not require as much testosterone as before so their bodies naturally produce less of it.

The huge sports world that continues to celebrate male strength and speed was once a private preserve of males. It is now co-ed. When female sports figures outdo their male counterparts the news media glorifies their victory and notes that their accomplishments prove women can be the equal, if not better, than men when they have the opportunity.

It is entirely possible that if the present trend for women to get bigger and stronger and to engage in dangerous and demanding activities (like fighting in wars!) continues over several generations, and the trend for men over the same timeframe is the exact opposite, the paramount role of the sexes could be reversed.

One thing that would speed up this trend, for both males and females, would be for more and more women to opt for artificial insemination to get pregnant rather than take the old fashion sweaty way. The final straw that would surely herald the end of men as cocks-of-the-walk will be the day in the not-so-distant future when enough women decide they don't want to go through the inconvenience of pregnancy and the pain of childbirth, and relegate those functions to baby-producing labs.

In any event, the cultural juggernaut that is now diminishing the stud role of American men and in-creasing the male role of American women has achieved self-perpetuating size, weight and speed, and will inevitably play itself out.

[13]
The Role of Languages in Human Cultures!

One aspect of the failure of parenting and education in the U.S. that has contributed so much to the overall destruction of moral standards has to do with language.

There are obviously several factors in the creation of languages that make them unique, and these cultural-laden factors are not the result of conscious planning. They evolve naturally from a variety of influences that fashion and control the lifestyles of the people involved.

To fully understand and know a people you must be intimately familiar with the key words in their native languages that control their thinking and behavior—a fact of incredible importance that has not yet become common knowledge even among scholars and educators, much less diplomats, politicians and the international business com-munity.

Incredibly, the relationship between languages and cultural behavior is still only dimly perceived or is ignored altogether, with the result that the world is continuously roiled by misunderstandings, friction and violence.

Still today only a few American educators have even achieved enough common sense to recognize that babies and toddlers can be exposed to and learn two or languages at the same time, and that instead of damaging or restricting their intellectual develop-ment it can make them smarter and give them a much broader, innate understanding of other people.

Mainstream Americans in particular have tra-ditionally been insensitive to the languages and cultures of other countries. Broadly speaking this failing, which is certainly not limited to Americans, is a result of prejudices built into the different cultures and manifested in culturally pregnant terms in the languages concerned.

The New Language Generation Gap

During a recent lunch-break when surfing TV channels I came across a show that featured males in their late teens and twenties. I could understand only about 50 percent of what they said—a cultural phenomenon that was recognized in Japan in the 1970s by a noted sociologist who referred to the younger generation as *Shin Jin Rui* [Sheen Jeen Ruuey], or "New Breed of People."

This same phenomenon had, of course, also become common in other plugged-in countries around the world—even attracting attention in China by the turn of the century.

What has not and is not being seriously considered by most parents, educators and the public at large is the fact that languages are both the repository of cultures and the vehicle by which they are sustained and passed on to succeeding generations.

All of the key values and guidelines of cultures—the good and bad—are found in key words of the respective languages—terms that I refer to as "cultural code words" in my books on the business practices, cultures and overall mindset of the Chinese, Japanese, Koreans and Mexicans.

During my early years as a journalist in Asia beginning in 1949 I found that the cultures of every country in the region were bound up in key words in their languages, and that these key terms served as doorways to understanding and working within these cultures.

This experience made it obvious that all cultures are language-bound and the only way to truly understand them is to learn the cultural content, in all of its nuances, of key words in the languages concerned.

Explaining the Japanese term *kata* [kah-tah], for example, required a whole book: *KATA – The Key to Understanding and Dealing with the Japanese.* One could also write a book on the full meanings and uses of hundreds of individual words in Chinese— *palu* [pah-luu], for example, which refers to "virtue vs. the law."

My series of "cultural code word" books on China, Japan, Korea and Mexico contain detailed explanations of several hundred key words in the respective languages. They are all available from Amazon.

The point is that younger generations in the plugged-in nations of the world are creating new dialects of their languages—dialects that have their own cultural content that is not understandable to older generations.

The words in these new dialects reflect the mind-set—the new morality—of the young people who created them; not the values of the older generations. This is a major factor in the degeneration of the best elements of traditional cultures, and has serious implications for the future that for the most part is being ignored by older adults in general.

Many of the new attitudes and forms of behavior that have surfaced and grown since the "social revolutions" that began in the 1950s are major contributors to the problems now facing all facets of American society. If this rapidly developing trend continues unabated these problems can only intensify.

Not all of the new culture that has emerged in the U.S. since the 1950s is bad, but much of it is and until the dangers it represents are recognized by parents, educators, employers *and the news media,* and practical steps taken to stop the trend and re-educate those who now speak only the new truncated dialect, the negative side of this Orwellian "new speak" will continue to grow.

How to Export Democracy

American politicians, diplomats and others are obsessed with exporting democracy to non-democratic countries around the world...but they have traditionally gone about it in half-hearted and often wrong ways.

The easiest, fastest and cheapest ways to export the best American ideals of democracy is to export the best and the most powerful words in the American language—those that incorporate equality, fairness, justice, the rule of law, etc., in their cultural content.

In other words, we should be exporting the best of our language instead of weapons and war. You teach people, in any country, the best words in the English language and their mindset is forever changed...and little by little their behavior changes as well.

If you want other people to understand Americans and to begin to think and behave like Americans teach them the American language as it was spoken before the advent of the present culture of gross entertainment and mass media.

***

To repeat an old truism that is even more evident today:
In politics stupidity is not a handicap!

—Napoleon Bonaparte—

***

[14]
Challenges
Facing Mankind!

To recap, it is patently obvious that male-created religious doctrines designed to control the sexual behavior of females have had unforeseen results that made the lives of both men and women a travesty of their nature.

One of the most disastrous of the measures imposed upon both men and women but especially women was limiting sexual behavior to the point that most individuals spent much of their lives in a state of sexual frustration caused by a build-up of sexual energy that could not be expended.

Until contemporary times even masturbation, especially by males, was regarded as a major sin against God and was punished by a variety of means, including things that were demeaning and often cruel.

The results of this misunderstanding and misuse of human sexuality included both emotional and physical ailments that still today continue plague much of mankind and historically have also resulted in thriving prostitution industries in most countries.

It is also just now finally being recognized by a few authorities that unused sexual energy in males is responsible for much of the violence in societies.

When education and other forms of enlightenment began to loosen some of the religious restraints on sexual attitudes and behavior in the United States, businessmen were quick to pick up on and exploit the area of human sexuality that was the most abused, most constrained—and that, of course, was female sexuality.

Advertisements began to feature attractive women in seductive poses and various states of undress. By the 1950s most marketing programs in the country were based on the prurient appeal of female sexuality. And in the following decades female sexuality-related advertisements began to appear in Japan and other Asian countries.

Well before the end of the 20th century the level of sexuality portrayed in American advertisements of all kinds and in every medium had reached the level of soft pornography. By the beginning of the 21st century many marketing programs had reached the level of semi-hard porn to attract attention to products...and hard-core porn had become a staple of movies and television shows.

Another fallout from the misunderstanding and misuse of human sexuality is the declining custom of marriage and the increase in children born out of wedlock...both of which have a powerful, negative effect on the stability of societies and the quality of life.

By the turn of the century the economic impact of single parent families among minorities and especially illegal immigrants.—all of whom qualified for government handouts of cash, rebates and food stamps—had become one of the largest tax burdens in the U.S.

The sexual revolution that now encompasses much of humanity—again caused by the mostly well-intentioned attempts of religious doctrines to limit sexual behavior and channel it into narrow confines—is still in its early stages. Where and how far it will go remains to be seen but it cannot be allowed to run the course set for it by the present profit-at-any-cost based morality.*

---

*I have presented evidence for several possible scenarios in my novelized account of sex in America: **EROS' REVENGE – Brave New World of American Sex!,** avail-able from Amazon. Many of these scenarios have already come true and others are on their way. First written in the 1960s, the book has been updated several times to cover predictions that have come true.

Of course, striving to transform the many cultures of the world and create a global Earth Culture is a challenge of epic proportions. In addition to the religious obstacles, there is the automobile industry, the oil industry, and the use of sex as the foundation of the advertising, marketing and entertainment industries—all of which fly in the face of common sense.

The profits involved in the automobile and oil industries alone virtually rule the world, and in today's world profit comes before morality, before sanity, and especially before the future! It goes without saying that these two industries are not going to change their stripes anytime soon! They will surely milk the oil and automobile cows as long as it is profitable—or at least until they have managed to come up with other ways of producing energy and transportation modes that allow them to continue to control much of the economies of the world.

The blatant, gross use of sex in business is another of the most negative legacies of the religious distortion and repression of the sexual impulse.

Even once straight-laced Asian countries have picked up on the American way of using sex to sell. This misuse and abuse of human sexuality is also not going to go away until we manage to create a new ethic for sexual behavior that is rational, satisfying and doable.

As already noted, we also need to obliterate the religious doctrines that continue to contribute to unsustainable population growth. Neither planet

Earth nor "God" needs more people, and the Church-based obsession that "He" does is another kind of pathological insanity!

Furthermore, the religious/economic-political concept that prosperity and the quality of life are based on a continuously growing population is not only outdated, it is one of the primary factors in the poverty that plagues over half of the population of the Earth, including millions of people in the most prosperous nations.

Over-population is also one of the primary sources of much of the violence that afflicts so much of mankind. In fact, the world needs some kind of parental code of ethics that people be required to agree to before they have children—in or outside of wedlock. To start with, courses in parenting responsibilities and skills should be made a mandatory part of the education of the young.

The political, economic and social policies of promoting growth and more growth just for the sake of growth and for political and religious power must be eliminated from the human mindset. Economic growth should first of all be designed to raise the level of the living standard of all people on Earth to a comfortable level while ensuring that it is sustainable both during the process and afterward.

All of the prevailing reasons why men go to war—religion, the hunger for political power, the obsession with wealth, territorial ambitions, oppressive government regimes—should be eliminated by a coordinated universal effort that now seems to be so far beyond the ability of mankind that it is not even a dream. But that is exactly what at least 95 percent of the people on Earth want! So why can't it be done?

It *can* be done but it will not be done until religious and political leaders are no longer in the dark ages where ignorance, irrationality and inhuman behavior are the norm—the norm for them; not for the people at large.

One factor that has already raised the living standard of people in China and India—two countries that represent two-thirds of humanity—is work out-sourced from the United States, Japan, South Korea and other developed countries…a phenomena that began with Japan in the 1950s and from there spread to Hong Kong, Korea, Taiwan and Singapore.

As controversial and as painful to some as this phenomena is, it nevertheless is the most efficient and practical means of quickly achieving economic parity between nations—not tearing any of them down, but building all of them up.

The more affluent developing countries become, the more they contribute to the economies of the countries out-sourcing to them, the more stable their governments, and the more likely they are to cherish and work for peace and prosperity.

Of course, there are many other things that should be done. And despite all of the gloom and doom scenarios I've harped on the great majority of people on this endangered planet are good-hearted, well-behaved and hard-working, and want only to live peaceful, comfortable, secure lives.

The truly evil doers—those leaders and their henchmen who are actually well-known to the world—number only in the thousands. If the world could somehow get rid of them and prevent others from taking their place the Earth could and surely would become a sane, safe habitat for humanity in a very short period of time.

The material quality of life is primarily deter-mined by knowing what to do and having the political and religious freedom to do it. This makes it imperative that all people be freed from the destructive religious, political and economic shackles of the past.

[15]
Solutions for the
Sexual Needs of Males
And Females!

Everywhere you look there are powerful images and signs of the dysfunction of cultures—much of which could be eliminated by the creation of a practical solution for the sexual needs of males and females, beginning at the age of puberty.

One of the oldest and most conspicuous symptoms of dysfunctional cultures is that of prostitution. As the ancient axiom indicates, prostitution is one of if not the oldest profession on the planet.

Why is this so? It all goes back to the fact that humanity has not come up with a fair and practical way of dealing with the sexual needs of males and the way women have been relegated to a subservient role in the sexual affairs of humanity.

The only way single males, widowed males, males whose wives did not or could not keep them sexually satiated, or married males who still reacted to the primitive urge to fornicate with multiple females, could even partially fill their sexual needs—real or imagined— has been and still is to go to prostitutes.

And this despite the fact that many cultures have promoted or condoned multiple non-professional female partners for men in the form of concubines and mistresses, and now, just plain girl friends.

In all Asian countries where the religions legally permitted men to have more than one sexual partner prostitution still flourished, at least until recent times if not today. In Japan, for example, official red-light districts were a major and conspicuous part of the landscape until 1956, when they were ordered closed after newly elected female members of the Diet demanded that they be banned. Managers in the industry were given one year to get out of the business.*

---

*The largest and most elaborate red-light district in Japan was the famous Yoshiwara in the Asakusa district of Tokyo at the end of the Ginza Subway Line. I and two of my friends went there on the last night of its existence—the eve of April Fools' Day, 1957.

In addition to the hundreds of such official districts throughout the country, the thousands of inns that flourished during the long Tokugawa Shogun era [1603-1867] had female partners available for male travelers. In fact, it was the official policy of the

Tokugawa government that married men should not be deprived of sexual release when they were away from home.

Of course, the banning of legal red-light districts in Japan did not end the practice of organized prostitution. It simply adapted to the new circumstances, moving into massage parlors and other legitimate venues.

The sexual practices in African, Middle Eastern and European nations have all included prostitution in various forms since ancient times—some fully sanctioned by the governments, and others tolerated because the ruling male elite unofficially approved of them.

Moslem countries have traditionally attempted to circumvent the role of prostitutes by making it legal for men to have multiple wives, but even this did not mean the end of prostitution.

In the U.S. today prostitution is legal in only a few places, but it is practiced in one form or another in every city in the country. City police will occasionally round up street prostitutes if they become too conspicuous and there are too many complaints, and they sometimes raid massage parlors that offer sexual services, but the industry survives and thrives.

May actors, businessmen and politicians are known to be regular patrons of prostitutes, but it generally doesn't raise an eyebrow unless a well-known figure is involved and some kind of scandal occurs—and then the news media jumps in and repeats over and over every lurid detail it can find, helping to promote the sex industry—it having been reveal again and again that attempts by religious leaders and others to eliminate prostitution and porn shops increases rather than decreases the volume of the sex business.

And now, of course, there is the Internet, with the Constitution of the United States guaranteeing the right of Americans to produce, promote and sell pornography and sexual implements—all of which pro-motes the variety and volume of sexual activity in the country.

I have maintained for decades that the most practical and efficient solution to the problem of providing adult males and females with sexual partners when they need or want them is to license individual adult women and men to provide sexual services on a commercial basis.

Licenses could be issued to men and women who are not married and above the age of consent, to divorcees, and to widows and to widowers—a solution that would dramatically reduce the buildup of sexual energy in both males and females, and provide gainful employment for hundreds of thousands—if not millions—of people.

What a boon to the service industry this would be—and just image the income from licensing fees…which could, at least for a while, reach the level of government income from tobacco and alcohol.

Both males and females become sexually potent at puberty, which is increasingly at a younger and younger age because like other life forms the physiology of human beings change with changing circumstances—just like Darwin's animals, fish and fowls.

Sexual potency is at its peak in both males and females from the age of puberty to around the mid-20s, and both expecting and forcing them to refrain from sexual intercourse until they get married is both ir-rational and harmful in many ways. The solution to this real problem is simply to formally and officially allow young unmarried males and females to have intimate relationships as soon as they are old enough to take the responsibility necessary for them to avoid pregnancies and venereal diseases.

These practices would eliminate most of the sexual stress that afflicts younger unmarried males and fe-males; it would help prevent these same people from growing up to have a variety of harmful sexual hang-ups; it would hopefully also eliminate most of the obsession with sexual titillation that now passes as entertainment…and it could help teens become more responsible adults in their sexual relationships.

The facts are, of course, that young males and females in some countries, including the United States, are already creating this new paradigm on their own, with or without the approval of their parents, other adults, and institutions of whatever kind.

Still another suggestion is that married men and women could agree to be free to have civilized, harmonious affairs with other partners without any negative influence on their marriage—something that would no doubt roil the "me-only" ego of many males. But the positive benefits of this customs could be miraculous. Men who didn't want to lose their wives would be better husbands. Women who didn't want to lose their husbands would be better wives.

Surprising to some, perhaps, this trend is well underway. Surveys in 2010 showed that around one-third of American married men and women over the age of 40 were having extra-marital affairs, and a larger percentage thought it was a good idea.

Of course, men and women who did not have spouses would be free to have mutually consensual intimate relation-ships with anyone of their choice— also already a growing reality in the U.S. and elsewhere.

If these practices were followed, there would be far less sexual frustration among both men and women, the tendency for male violence would be drama-tically reduced, and the world would be a saner, happier place.

The time is long past when religions and other institutions that don't work in the first place should be eliminated as the controllers of the sexual behavior of human beings. There is nothing sacred or profane about sex. It is simply the way life works, and when this natural process is denied or perverted problems are inevitable.

[16]
The Need for a New
Cultural Paradigm!

Mankind is now faced with new challenges spawned by anger at the stupidity and idiocy of traditional cultures. In the U.S. and elsewhere this anger has led to the misuse of technology to create new cultures that in some respects are worse than the old ones.

It obviously goes without saying that to truly meet the physical, emotional, intellectual and spiritual needs of mankind the world needs a new, global, cultural paradigm—one that "fits" and enhances the lives of everybody in all societies.

But are there principles and policies that would ensure high standards of ethical behavior and would work on a worldwide basis?

I believe there are, but to create and implement this new paradigm would mean discarding all of the institutionalized and ritualized one-God cult religions... and again if you question my calling Judaism, Christianity and Islam "cults," look up the word "cult" yourself in your dictionary! The only difference between these three cults and notorious little cults is that these three are very big and very powerful, and can ignore and squash criticism.

It is, of course, a fact that some of the social tenets of Judaism and Christianity are responsible for much of the humane morality that has managed to survive in the United States and other Western count-ries. But even the most casual measurement of the level of morality in so-called Christianized societies reveals that corruption and immoralities of all kinds are thriving as never before.

A *Letter to the Editor* written by a woman that appeared in this morning's *Arizona Republic* newspaper described the lack of morals in the U.S. as appalling... a response that, of course, could have been carved into stone during the Stone Age, long before the Big Three religions were created.

And then the letter writer goes on to say that the only way this appalling problem can be solved is for the Christian God to do it—as if a god actually had anything to do with the idiocies and depredations of mankind.

Of course, Christianity now presents itself as humane and nurturing. But it is still off-base in many of its teachings—and has never been and is not now capable of instilling a desirable standard of morality even in "Christianized" countries, much less universally.

Islam is even worse—at least in some respects. It remains caught in a time warp, with many of the same irrational and barbarous tenets that were the bedrock of Christianity for many centuries—the same Christianity that was responsible for the crusades against Muslims, for the Catholic Inquisitors who tortured and burned thousands over a period of several generations, for the depredations of the Conquistadors in the New World, for the European Colonialists and their campaigns to subjugate native populations in Africa and to eradicate them in North and South America, and on and on.

And there is another very conspicuous obstacle to the creation and implementation of a new code of ethics for humanity. This obstacle is a large number of professional people world-wide in think tanks, in universities, and in other organizations that have agendas that range from being anti-white, anti-black, anti-Jewish, anti-Islamic, anti-democratic, anticapitalism, anti-globalism, anti-American, to anti-international business, and more.

As is also obvious, these groups now have the means to reach millions of people daily with their virulent messages. A recent book entitled *Welcome to the Ivory Tower of Babel* by Michael Adams presents a fascinating and frightening portrait of these think-tank and campus-based anti-every-thing groups.

[17]
Guidelines for a New Cultural Paradigm

So what might a new social paradigm look like—one that all people could live by and achieve their fullest potential? Being as practical as possible, given what is known about humanity, the new cultural paradigm would have to include the following elements:

1) That all governments be based on the best principles of democracy.

2) That all societies acknowledge and follow the fundamental principle that females have an equal stake in humanity and must have the same rights and same opportunities as males.

3) That morality is based on dogma-free principles that recognize the true nature of mankind and are designed to nurture all of the elements in the make-

up of human beings: the body, the emotions, the intellect and the spirit.

4) That the educational policies of all governments and all educational institutions be redesigned to inculcate all students from day one with a genteel standard of etiquette; a moral value system that includes respect for others, honesty, truthfulness and diligence; a sense of pride in themselves; a sense of honor; the ambition to make the world a better place; and the courage to have big dreams.

5) That the economic policies of all governments be re-formed to further a global-based process of raising the living standards of all people on the planet to a comfortable level.

6) That the finite nature and fragility of Planet Earth be totally recognized and that universal mandatory directives be established to protect and sustain it... balanced with the profit-making that is essential for the well-being of humanity.

7) That these goals be made the basic charter of man-kind and be pursued on a global, coordinated basis.

Of course, there are hundreds of other factors, real and imagined, that would have to be a part of this paradigm shift. What I am saying is that all societies on the planet must become inter-connected to the point that they are, in fact, members of a global society. An old idea…a global village!

We've gone from a Cold War of political ideologies to a Hot War of religious ideologies. And that is the new reality of the 21st century. We must therefore strive with everything in our power to bring all countries into the same rational, logical, humane, human family.

And the United States, despite its many short-comings, is the best hope for leading the world in a crusade for a sane, rational, comprehensive, universal morality. Much of the world is, in fact, waiting for us to create and demonstrate a morality that would lift mankind up and out of the religious, political and economic muck and mire of history.

We have very obviously already attempted to start this crusade. But we have failed to do enough of the educational groundwork necessary to bring the mass of humanity on board the effort, even in the United States!

I fault all of the Establishments for this failure: the Political Establishment; the Business Establishment, and most of all, the Educational Establishment. I could have added Religious Establishments, but all of them have already failed in every facet of their self-proclaimed mandates.

The Educational Establishment is the guiltiest of all in failing to provide a foundation for a truly humane and ethical world society because the majority of educators know—or should know—what is good for humanity and what is not good!

But most of the people making up the Educational Establishments worldwide, like people in many political institutions, are more self-serving than society-serving—not all by choice but by the systems we've created. Furthermore, both academia and religions have always attracted active zealots whose goals often do not serve mankind.

Of course, there is already a lot of complaining and wailing about these systems. But like religious and political institutions, the educational organizations are too divided, too hemmed in by laws, too entrenched, and too bureaucratic to reform themselves.

> The trouble with the world
> is that the stupid are cocksure
> and the intelligent
> are full of doubt!
>
> —*Bertrand Russell*—

[18]
The Fate Facing
Earth and Mankind!

There are now nearly seven billion human beings on planet Earth. It is the judgment of experts in many fields that three billion people—less than half of the present number—would be an adequate and sustainable figure.

What is even more telling and frightening is the estimate that at the present rate of growth the number of people on the planet will double in the next 50 or 60 years. Given the damage that has already been done to the planet since the Industrial Age began in the early 1800s an additional six or seven billion people looms as a doomsday scenario.

As of this writing [2010] one half of all of the oxygen-making forests that existed in 1800 have been destroyed; one half of all of the grasslands that existed at that time have also been destroyed. The pace of this destruction is increasing each year to accommodate and feed more people. The race and tribal factors that have fed civil wars and genocide in a number of African countries is one symptom of this competition for exclusive rights to land.

To make this image more complete, only some 30 percent of the Earth's surface is land. Of this mass, one-third is comprised of sheets of ice around the North and South Poles. Only one-fourth of the ice-free land is even remotely livable—and the melting of the ice sheet around the North Pole will not change this situation.

If the size of population is not controlled it could result in a nightmare scenario that one might see in a horror movie: hundreds of millions or even billions of people living on floating platforms on the Earth's oceans and seas...that have become cesspools of waste.

But there are more immediate concerns. Pressure from the expanding population is destroying not only forests and grasslands it is also slowly but surely poisoning the oceans, causing the extinction of hundreds to thousands of life forms each year on land and in the seas.

In 2010 the National Research Council of the U.S. released findings revealing that one million tons of carbon dioxide are being absorbed by the world's oceans *every hour of the day*—and that the oceans are now 30 percent more acidic than they were before the Industrial Revolution began in the early 1800s, and that the impact on coral and sea life has already be-come serious.

The scientists predicted that the acidic content of the oceans will increase by 200 percent by the end of this century, and even more in the next century if the rate of carbon dioxide production continues to grow.

The Human Threat to Animal Life

The primitive id-based urge for human males to kill wild animals, originally for food but now for sport and profit, has already destroyed some of the world's largest animal herds in North America, Africa and Asia. Last year [2009] in one area of Africa alone Preserve guards found and confiscated 70,000 traps set for animals by poachers.

Male hunters continue to kill hundreds of thou-sands of animals each year for sport—in many cases as part of official government programs to keep their numbers down because larger numbers interfere with the lives of people.

In other words, in today's world humans have the right to live and propagate without restraint but animals do not. There is something wrong with that one-sided view of the world.

The religious and economic rationales used to justify the present population growth rate and the destruction of the Earth's plant and animal life are anti-human as well as anti-Earth. This goes beyond being stupid. It is a kind of perverse insanity.

Of course, there are literally millions of people who are aware of this destruction and hundreds of thousands who have been speaking out against it for decades but the system is so large and so powerful and their efforts have been miniscule.

In 2010 the Supreme Court of the United States de-creed that the Freedom of Speech provision in the Bill of Rights gives human beings the right to kill, maim and otherwise treat animals cruelly when presented as entertainment.

The Power of Technology

Since the beginning of the Industrial Revolution in England around 1800 the rapid appearance of new technology has done more to change both the behavior and mindset of human beings than anything else since the dawn of human history—and, in fact, is rapidly becoming the new God.

Since the last decades of the 20th century there have been many extraordinary examples of the power of technology to inspire people and change their think-ing. These examples have included science fiction movies and television fare—especially *Star Trek*, which was a preview of the kind of future everyone should and could have.

There are now millions of people who are concerned about the welfare of the planet because of what they have seen and heard in movies and on television, and more and more of them have become active in the growing efforts to protect and present the Earth.

Television has, of course, become the greatest force in making millions of people aware of the threats to the planet. Among this TV fare are two recently produced documentary films that go beyond the incredible in their revelation of the diversity, the sweep, and the beauty of the Earth and its life forms.

These films include *Planet EARTH*, produced by the British Broadcasting Corporation [BBC] in 2007; [with the U.S. version narrated by James Earl Jones, the UK version by Patrick Stewart, the German version by Ulrich Tukur, and the Japanese version by Ken Watanabe]; and *Disney's OCEANS*, released by Disney in 2010, and narrated by Pierce Brosnan.

No one can view these films without being stirred to the depths of their being by the images of the Earth and its life forms, and surely inspired to add their voices to the imperative of protecting and preserving the Earth.

Former Vice-President Al Gore had already raised the awareness of the fragility of the Earth and the potentially deadly affects of human generated pollution with his film *An Inconvenient Truth*, released in 2006, and in subsequent speeches he made worldwide.

Unfortunately, and in ways that once again emphasizes both the ignorance and willful stupidity of many people, there was a chorus of criticism aimed at Gore, saying his sources of information about the warming of the Earth were faulty, that he skewered some of his "facts" to reach his conclusions, and that temperatures colder than usual in different parts of the Earth belied his conclusions.

These critics totally ignored indisputable evidence of the melting ice-cap at the top of the Earth, the rapid disappearance of glaciers all over the world, and the warming of the oceans.

Many of the critics say "going green" would result in the disappearance or down-sizing of many industries and have a seriously negative impact on the economies worldwide. It has been repeatedly demonstrated that "going green" would create more jobs than it destroyed.

[19]
Saving
Earth and Humanity!

The common sense of females, the power of technology and a growing number of enlightened males now offer mankind an opportunity to solve what is potentially one of the greatest problems human beings have ever faced—how to get population growth under control and create a new universal cultural paradigm.

Attempts to prevent pregnancy in females go back at least three thousand years [and included some far out methods], but nothing really worked well until the development of the Pill in 1950s by American scientists, and its approval by the Food and Drug Administration in 1960. At that time the typical American woman had 3.6 children.

Just one pill a day was effective over 92 percent of the time in preventing pregnancy. Side effects were rare [and have since been virtually eliminated]. When first introduced each pill cost only 12 cents.

At that time, attempts to prevent pregnancy were banned by a number of religions and there were actually laws in various religions-oriented states and countries making family planning a criminal offense.

First, women by the thousands began taking the tiny pill daily, despite the laws and religious edicts, and their numbers continued to grow. By 1980 the birth rate among white Americans had dropped below two for the first time in the history of the country.

Despite the fact that the primitive bastions of male power kept up the battle year after year to prevent women from taking the Pill, their numbers soon passed a million, then ten million and by 2010 well over one hundred million.

The gradual unfolding of this pregnancy revolution by American women was chronicled by *TIME* magazine in 2010, revealing a battle that started several thousand years ago, and is still only in its early stage.

Some of the methods used in an effort to prevent pregnancy in ancient times were bizarre to say the least—including such things as the male putting a ring made from a cut lemon around his penis.

In 1873 the American Congress passed a law labeling birth-control information obscene and banning its distribution to the public.

Well into the 20th century contraception of any kind was opposed by orthodox religions around the world, the most powerful of which even regarded sex within marriage as immoral unless it was aimed at having children. Families with up to 14 or more children were widely praised and held up as paragons of moral behavior.

Women who first women began the push for birth-control methods, including some Catholic women, were treated as criminals. Margaret Sanger, one of the first major figures in this battle, took up the fight after her mother died from complications caused by 18 pregnancies.

She wrote that she dreamed of a "magic pill." She was arrested and spent time in jail for her efforts.

Not surprisingly, the man who was ultimately responsible for the development of the Pill began his research in an effort to *increase fertility in women who were having trouble conceiving*—not blocking pregnancies!

The emancipation of American women from getting pregnant every 21 or 22 months was to have a profound influence on the social and economic situation of females, resulting in them swarming into universities and corporate offices by the millions.

By the end of the 20th century some lower level religious leaders had bowed to the inevitable and given grudging approval of the Pill for married women—or they kept quiet about it because they knew large numbers of their members had been using it for many years.

The Political Push Back

Still today there is tremendous opposition to the Pill by critics in some African countries who say it is being used as a political weapon by the White race to limit the number of Blacks—and by dogged conservative politicians in the United States who claim the moral high ground by opposing unnatural contraception.

But as history has proven over and over again, nothing changes human behavior faster and more completely than new technology that makes life easier and better. Technology that has benefits that are immediately obvious changes physical behavior virtually instantly—*and a change in thinking inevitably follows.*

Saving the Earth for Humanity!

The most important—the most vital—of the steps that must be taken to protect and preserve the Earth and its life forms is to make family planning universal and mandatory on a world-wide basis.

It goes without saying that this is a cultural challenge the likes of which many countries have never faced before. But not meeting the challenge is too horrible to contemplate.

There is, of course, a precedent for this challenge, and that is China, where in 1979 supreme leader Deng Xiao-ping decreed that couples in urban areas of the country could not have more than one child in a desperate measure to stop the ballooning of the population that had already exceeded one billion.

Deng was able to make this draconian policy stick because he had absolute control of the country and did not face the wrath of religious zealots whose God demands that couples have as many children as is physically possible—a practice that traditionally has been more acceptable to men than to women.

In advanced and developing countries the reduction in population growth rate is underway because a growing number of couples are making the decision on their own, regardless of their religious affiliations.

This movement is based on immediate economic factors as well as on a growing awareness that large families are not as desirable as they used to be. But it is far below what is necessary to lower the overall population of the Earth.

Still, it has been shown repeatedly that when wives in poverty-stricken countries are provided with the means to avoid multiple pregnancies many of them will do so—a very hopeful sign.

But achieving a negative birthrate will require a combination of government will on an international basis and a fundamental change in the position of religions that promote large families because it is "God's will."

In fact, the world needs some kind of parenting code of ethics that people be taught before they get married and have children—in or outside of wedlock. To start with, courses in parenting responsibilities and skills should be made a mandatory part of the education of the young. But there must be more. There must be a universal family planning program that brings rationality and practicality into pro-creation.

One of the most critical factors in American society that makes the population problem even more pressing is the preponderance of single women, particular Blacks and Hispanics, who have children—something that has developed because of sexually aggressive and irresponsible males and a government system of supporting single parents.

[In earlier times in Catholic Mexico one of the prerogatives of upper class males was to impregnate any number of lower class single females...a practice also followed by white owners of black slaves in early America.]

The political, economic and social policies of promoting growth and more growth for the sake of profit and power must be eliminated from the human mind-set. Economic growth should first of all be designed to raise the level of the living standard of all people on Earth to a comfortable level that it is sustainable.

The battle for women's right to control the number of children they have is far from over. Individual religious zealots in the private sector as well as many who are in public office are keeping the fight going by opposing family planning in any form or fashion—with many resorting to mental and physical intimidation, and some to murder.

As of this writing national polls show that over two-thirds of young American males and females believe that the ability to prevent unwanted pregnancies is important, but 63 percent say they know very little about birth control pills, and much of what they say they know is wrong.

All public institutions and organizations, including the religions, should join together to make the Pill available to females worldwide. Each Pill costs only a few cents to produce, and they could be made avail-able for free-pickup in places in every city, town, village and rural area in the world.

But the responsibility of controlling the population of the Earth should not and will not be left up to females alone. As of 2010 dramatic advances had been made by American scientists in the development of new means of preventing conception for both women and men.

For women these new methods include jells, and a ring for insertion into the vagina that is effective for one year. Contraceptive methods for men include long-lasting pills, injections and patches placed on the skin.

Whether or not males make use of this new techno-logy will be the ultimate test of their concern, both for their female partners and the Earth.

For this to happen there would have to be a significant rise in the intelligence and knowledge of several billion people in the under developed as well as the developed regions of the planet.

This is not going to happen for decades if not centuries given the level of social development around the world.

[20]
Technology as Both
God *and* Satan!

Given all the negative influences in today's cultures, the only salvation for humanity may be the positive influence of technology—which by itself is already rapidly changing all of the world's cultures. In the long run, even without courageous forward thinking and forward-acting leaders, the world's cultures will be-come more and more rational, and more and more democratic because of the incomparable ability of technology to inform, to educate, to encourage critical thinking and to change the behavior of people—and especially to influence people to demand their natural rights to be free and secure.

But given the fact that primitive religions and authoritarian political forms still have a death-grip on the majority of mankind, these transformations could take generations—time the Earth does not have—because leaders will not or cannot take the heroic steps necessary to change today's morality and today's policies even if they *want* these things to happen!

And, of course, there are regional and national leaders who are dead-set against such freedom and against a humane morality for the people they rule. As a result, many people may continue to be oppressed and prevented from achieving their full potential for generations to come unless these changes are aggressively promoted by huge numbers of people blogging the world's bureaucrats and leaders in business, in politics and in religions with criticism and advice! And even more importantly, by simply refusing to go along with stupid, insane policies and by voting the people who promote them out of office!

Of course, there are thousands of things one can point to in the U.S. and elsewhere that are en-couraging. I saw in a recent news article that American entrepreneurs have established etiquette schools to teach young kids basic, good manners, something that parents used to do in their homes.

But how many schools that teach manners and the ac-companying morality do you think it will take and how long will it take to counter all of the coarse behavior and lack of ethics that are being pro-grammed into the minds of millions of children and young people seven days and nights a week by the so-called entertainment industries?

Of course, the majority of people everywhere are sickened by all of these cultural failures. But survival, power and profit-making...not moral behavior...are the overwhelming goals of most leaders in politics and business. And as already said, there is no way that the weak, divided and often irrational spiritual-based moralities of today are going to change that!

We therefore need to teach and follow a philosophy of living and working that is based on common sense, on the fragile nature of the Earth, on the real physical, emotional, intellectual, spiritual and philosophical needs of human beings.

There are hundreds of thousands of people already espousing these philosophies but with so little impact that contemplating the future is frightening.

Despite the misuse and abuse of the Internet by hate mongers, pornographers and radical religious zealots—not to mention people who are simply ignorant—this new technology also makes it possible for the average person to make his or her voice heard on a large scale for the first time in the history of mankind.

Ordinary people can now vote and express themselves online at any time on very important issues of the day! If enough rational, educated, morally enlightened people will bring more and more pressure against leaders in every field to force them to give up their self-serving ways—or force them out of positions of authority and let a new breed of people have a go at it—the ancient religious promise of peace on earth might be achieved.

Two of the more obvious things that we in the United States are now talking about—and could do if we had the will—is to reintroduce discipline and a reality-based future-oriented curriculum into the educational system, and to boycott purveyors of obscene, immoral and harmful ideas and behavior instead of rewarding them with fame and great wealth.

Many Americans believe that freedom of religion, freedom of the press, freedom of assembly, and freedom of speech referred to in the First Amendment of the Constitution are constitutional rights...and that freedom of speech gives people the right to say or write almost anything, no matter how gross or false it might be.

But constitutional authority Robert Greenslade says that is not so. He says the sole purpose of the Bill of Rights was to add restraints to the powers of the federal government, and that the "rights" should be called the "Bill of Prohibitions" instead of the Bill of Rights.

The original purpose of the "Rights," Greenslade adds, was to reserve these rights to individuals as the "natural rights" of mankind rather than leave them in the hands of politicians.

As a result, the rights inherent in the individual amendments did not take into account the possibility that they could and might be abused.

It goes without saying that the Freedom of Speech provision in the First Amendments of the American Constitution should somehow be amended to prohibit its abuse by the so-called entertainment industries and others who abuse it for profit and power, without reducing the basic intent of the provision.

In addition to being morally inexcusable, the present extreme interpretations and use of the "Freedom of Speech" provision are socially insane.

As already said several times, it is the insatiable and irrational appetite for profit that controls the ethical and moral behavior of Americans and most other people in developed and developing nations. And again, the religious teaching that the pursuit of profit beyond real and justified needs is an evil has, or course failed, and is not going to change this human trait in the future.

That fundamental change in the nature of human beings will not occur until technology has reached the point that the creation of products and services can be automated and made totally free to consumers. At which point profit-making and money will no longer needed.

In the meantime, there are measures that can be taken to fundamentally change the behavior of people—measures that are based on the realities of life, not abstract religious teachings.

The Stupidity of Conspicuous Consumption

One of the greatest economic and social insanities that now control the lives of large numbers of people in advanced countries is a lifestyle based on over-consumption—buying and using, or buying and not using, products of all kinds that are far beyond actual needs.

Middle and upper class families typically have closets jam-packed with clothing that they seldom if ever wear. Many women have a dozen or more pairs of shoes. Useless dust collectors abound in many homes.

This conspicuous consumption is fueled by advertising that consciously and subconsciously convinces people—especially women—that they need all of these extra items to create and maintain an image that is important to their social standing and emotional well-being.

This artificially created image probably accounts for up to 60 or 70 percent of all apparel and cosmetic sales. Furthermore, the quality and durability of many of the apparel items is deliberately so low that they have very short lifetimes—a practice designed to ensure that they have to be replaced at relatively short intervals.

These social-economic factors obviously keep more people gainfully employed but they are an inexcusable waste of resources and a kind of make-work that belittles the value and potential of human beings. There has to be a better way.

More and more people are recognizing the stupidity and immorality of this kind of culture, but only a few have the intestinal fortitude in the first place to not fall prey to the blandishments of advertising and a social image that publicly proclaims their success in making more money than what they need to live modestly. Fewer still willingly give it up after they are caught up in the conspicuous consumption syndrome.

Americans created this lifestyle and mentality, and like a disease it has spread to other countries, particularly the newly developed and still developing countries, with China being an outstanding example.

China went from a bicycle economy to an auto-mobile economy between 1990 and 2010, when it became the world's largest market for auto-mobiles—not only for ordinary cars but also for the most expensive vehicles made. A 2010 business reported stated that automobile dealers in China had the largest back-log of orders for Rolls Royces the industry had ever seen for this famous luxury brand.

Japan was the first Asian nation to develop a mass market-based economy—between 1950 and 1965—a remarkable event chronicled by myself and my writer colleague Fred Thomas Perry in 1967 in our book, *The Japanese as Consumers—Asia's First Mass Market*.

Japan was also the first Asian nation to fall prey to the excess consumption syndrome; a cultural switch of extraordinary importance because up to 1960 the Japanese had maintained an austere but physically, emotionally and spiritually balanced lifestyle for over two thousand years.

This unique Japanese lifestyle evolved from precepts contained in Shintō, their native religion, which taught respect and reverence for nature; for beauty simplified and refined down to its essence; the avoidance of conspicuous display, and the presence of harmony in design and style as well as in behavior.

The traditional lifestyle of the Japanese has been maintained in many areas, including shops dealing in traditional arts and crafts, restaurants featuring traditional foods, and traditional *ryokan* [rio-kahn] or inns, which still abound in the country. But for the majority of the Japanese it has been replaced by the American or Western style of living.

However, before the turn of the 21st century a growing number of Japanese began to suffer from a cultural malaise brought on by the mass consumption lifestyle, resulting in them going at least part of the way back to the simple way of living that had sustained them for millennia. For some, this included moving out of crowded urban areas to the countryside.

Replacing Stupidity with Common Sense

It should not be surprising to Westerns caught up in mass consumption that the foundation of Japan's traditional lifestyle was emotional and spiritual harmony; the antithesis of mass consumption.

While it is inconceivable that large numbers of affluent Americans and other Westerners would give up their wasteful and discordant lifestyles readily and easily, it nevertheless is one way that would return common sense and harmony to their lives.

If you are interested in learning more about the foundation of Japan's traditional culture, see my book, *ELEMENTS OF JAPANESE DESIGN – Understanding and Using Japan's Classic Wabi-Sabi-Shibui Concepts,* available from Amazon.

Another move that would change your life dramatically would be to adopt the 26 principles and practices advocated Zen masters of India, China, Korea and Japan.

Enlightenment in the sense of the original Indian Zen master meant being able to recognize the difference between illusion and reality; between logical and illogical; between the rational and the irrational; between the practical and the impractical; between good and bad; between myth and reality, and so on— an understanding that has been difficult for the male sex to achieve since the origin of the human species.

The essence of the teachings of the founder of Zen Buddhism was that one does not need to study sacred texts, worship deities or engage in elaborate religious rituals to achieve enlightenment. Rather, one needs to break through the boundaries of such conventional thought using meditation and experiencing the world as it truly is in the moment.

Training in Zen

Buddhist monasteries that specialized in teaching the Zen way of life have their own internal community structures, and there are a variety of rituals and rules that help to generate a sense of community..

Some scholars have argued that the character of Zen philosophy lends itself to an amoral stance, or that Zen philosophy does not distinguish between good and evil. In contrast, others argue that those who see things as they really are—a goal of Zen practice— will naturally act morally.

Zen and Japan's Samurai

It was to be a class of warriors—the famous samurai of Japan's Shogun era [1192-1867/8]—that was to make Japan the premiere home of Zen and turn it into a comprehensive way of life for the ruling warriors.

Japan's samurai class began to evolve on a large scale following the establishment of the first Shogun form of government in 1192. The Shogun and all of the some 270 independent clan fief lords created their own armies of samurai warriors, forming a class that became hereditary.

By the 14th century this new class of samurai warriors had adopted Zen as its cultural guide-lines because of its emphasis on order, discipline and a precise morality that did not allow for any deviation.

The concepts taught by Zen became one of the foundations for the code of honor and behavior followed by the samurai—a code known as *Bushido* [Boo-she-doh], or "The Way of the Warrior."

Over the next 400-plus years the Zen-influenced principles and practices of the samurai were the law of the land. Zen masters and Zen schools thrived.

Japan's Zen masters taught that all humans have the capacity to attain enlightenment because we all have an inherent Buddha-nature; indeed, that we are all already enlightened beings, but our true potential has been clouded by ignorance.

Just as their ancient Indian predecessors had done Zen masters in Japan taught that the ignorance that plagued mankind could be overcome through meditation that resulted in a breakthrough in understanding the true nature of reality and our place in it—a process the Japanese called *satori* [sah-toh-ree], or the sudden achievement of enlightenment.

Different Zen sects in Japan developed various methods for achieving this enlightenment, with the most popular and common one being zazen [zah-zen] or "sitting" meditation. Za means a seat and refers to a cushion generally on a *tatami* [tah-tah-me], the thick reed-mats that traditionally covered floors in Japan [the veranda and hallways had wooden floors]. One of the more rigorous ways of striving for *satori* was to stand in the frigid water of a waterfall in winter-time.

Following its introduction into Japan Zen soon became a dominant force in Japanese cities and the countryside, influencing all of the common art forms and disciplines, including archery, architecture, calligraphy, interior decoration, landscaping, painting, product design and wearing apparel.

Zen, in fact, had a direct impact on all of the design and work-related activities in Japan. The goal of every artist, every craftsman, was to get down to the essence of the object or subject at hand, resulting in both beauty and functionality becoming the hallmarks of Japanese things.

This special quality of Japanese things became so common-place that Japanese did not consider it unusual. Everything they made, including simple household utensils, had the same quality.

Japan's traditional arts and crafts owed their special character to a merging of Shinto and Zen concepts of harmony, sensuality, spirituality and simplicity—a cultural factor that remains very much in evidence and in force among Japanese artists and craftsmen in present-day Japan.

The Shinto concept of harmony included the size and shape of things, how they were to be used, and their relationship with people. The spiritual element in Japanese things incorporated the essence and spirit of the materials used, and was based on both respecting and revering these inherent qualities.

The sensual element in Japanese arts and crafts was reflected by the things that people automatically find attractive—harmony in shape, in size, in the relationship of the parts, in the interaction of colors, in their feel when touched, and in the vibrations they project.

After generations of refining their designs and techniques, Japan's master artists and craftsmen achieved a kind and quality of beauty that trans-cended the obvious surface manifestations of their materials—a kind of beauty that was described as *yugen* (yuu-gane), meaning mystery or subtlety, that reflected the simplicity and honesty of Zen.

Quoting from my book *The Elements of Japanese Design*:

"*Yugen* beauty referred to a type of attractiveness— beneath the surface of the material but in delicate harmony with it—that registers on the conscious as well as the subconscious of the viewer. It radiates a kind of spiritual essence."

The skill and techniques that were going into Japan's arts and crafts by the 10th century became so deeply embedded in the culture that they were not distinguished from daily life, and were reflected in everything the Japanese did, from designing and building castles, gardens, homes and palaces to the creation of hand-made paper.

Despite the mostly Western façade that today's Japan presents to the world *yugen* beauty is still very much in evidence in the arts and crafts, in traditional restaurants, inns, wearing apparel shops, and else-where in many unexpected places.

Yugen is another Japanese word I recommend that other people learn and use because it clearly iden-tifies a concept that in other languages requires several sentences to explain—and in itself is an example of the traditional Japanese propensity to refine things down to their Zen essence.

This compulsive reduction tendency of the Japanese is also dramatically demonstrated in their ability to design and manufacture miniaturized hi-tech pro-ducts and use nano-technology to create new pro-cesses and new materials.

When the first Westerners of record stumbled onto Japan in the 1540s, the discovery of the islands resulted in an influx of foreign traders and Christian –missionaries, both groups intent on expanding their empires in Asia.

Among the many things that astounded these first European visitors to Japan was the incredible quality of its handicrafts and arts and the ability of Japanese craftsmen to copy any Western product not only perfectly but to improve on it in the process.

European traders who took up residence in Japan from the mid-1500s on began to ship large quantities of Japan's arts and crafts to the capitals of Europe, where many of them became collectors' items. Europeans found their aesthetic appeal both seductive and fascinating, and still today that appeal is one of the secrets of Japan's attraction to visitors from around the world.

As the generations passed, these institutions and rituals were further strengthened by the introduction of the Zen principles of dispensing with the superfluous and harmonizing life and nature, resulting in masters who could actually achieve virtual perfection in the arts and crafts.

Westerners who visit Japan even for a few days are invariably touched by this unique facet of Japanese culture.

Visitors to Japan do not have to go out of their way to experience this extraordinary influence of Japan's arts and crafts—and to take some of it home with them if they choose.

Still today the lodging experiences at these *shukubo* include the opportunity to participate in such traditional Buddhist practices as calligraphic copying sutras, and engaging in meditation under the guidance of temple priests.

Other activities at the *shukubo* temples include a fire ritual known as *goma* [go-mah] that is a symbolic way of burning away the excess earthly desires that build up in the human mind. This ritual is accompanied by Buddhist priests chanting sutras, giving it a mystical aura. Some of the temple lodges charge modest fees for participating in their rituals.

The purpose of the meditation ritual is to empty the mind of extraneous thoughts and focus all of one's awareness on the symbol of the primary Buddhist deity, and let the universal reality of Buddhism flow into one's life.

Emptying the mind of all of the external thoughts that constantly assail one is not as easy as you might think. Daizetsu Suzuki, one of Japan's most famous contemporary Zen Buddhist priests whom I had the great pleasure of meeting in Kamakura before he passed away, once said that the longest he had ever been able to totally free his mind of all thoughts was two and a half seconds.

Here are the 13 principles and 13 practices that were the foundation of the mindset and behavior of Japan's samurai class:

(1)
The Principle of
Duty & Human Kindness
Giri (ghee-ree) & *Ninjo* (neen-joh)

(2)
The Principle
of Setting Goals
Mokuteki
(Moh-kuu-tay-kee)

(3)

The Principle of Discipline

Kiritsu

(Kee-reet-sue)

(4)

The Principle of Perseverance

Tayumazu yaritsuzukeru

(Tah-yuu-mah-zuu yah-ree-t'sue-zuu-kay-ruu)

(5)

The Principle of Diligence

Kimben

(Keem-bane)

(6)

The Principle of Concentration

Shuchu

(Shuu-chuu)

(7)

The Principle of

Sharpening Your Mind

Ishiki

[Ee-she-kee]

(8)

The Principle of Repetition

Kurikaishi

(Kuu-ree-kigh-she)

(9)
The Principle of Awareness
Kizuite-Iru
(Kee-zoo-ee-tay-Ee-rue)

(10)
The Principle of Observing
Kizuki
(Kee-zuu-kuu)

(11)
The Principle of
Clearing the Mind
Mushin
(Muu-sheen)

(12)
The Principle of Honesty
Shojiki
(Shoh-jee-kee)

(13)
The Principle of Compassion
Dohjoh
(Dohh-johh)

****

(1)
The Practice of Manners
Gyogi
(G'yoh-ghee)

(2)
The Practice of Responsibility
Sekinin
(Say-kee-neen)

(3)
The Practice of Looking Good!
Mikaké
(Me-kah-kay)

(4)
The Practice of Keeping
Things in Order
Chitsujo
(Cheet-sue-joh)

(5)
The Practice of Paying Respect
Sonkei (Soan-kay-ee)
(6)
The Practice of
Appreciating Things
Kansha
(Kahn-shah)

(7)
The Practice of
Understanding Human Nature
Ningensei
(Neen-gane-say-ee)

(8)
The Practice of
Using Intuitive Intelligence
Chokkan
(Choke-kahn)

(9)
The Practice of
Using Emotional Intelligence
Kando
(Kahn-doh)

The phrase "emotional intelligence" was apparently coined in the 1990s by American author Daniel Goleman in a book by that name.
The concept of emotional intelligence was obviously not new in Western cultures but before Goleman identified it and gave it a name it was seldom if ever discussed as a specific topic and played no individual or separate role in the education system or in the personal or professional lives of people.

(10)
The Practice of
Using Cosmic Wisdom
Uchu / (Uu-chuuh)

(11)
The Practice of
Using the Power of "The Force"
Ki
(Kee)

(12)
The Practice of Harmony
Wa
(Wah)

(13)
The Practice of Tranquility
Wabi
(Wah-bee)

Part 3

You Can Become A Modern-Day Samurai

Zen is Not All "Other World" Stuff

The concept of Buddha-nature that would become central to Buddhist and Zen philosophy described a world in which all things are equal, and all are one with the cosmos.

Zen and other Buddhist sects have for many centuries engaged in efforts to improve the world around them, constructing bridges, building and running schools, hospitals, and other charitable endeavors. At times these were projects sponsored and carried out by monasteries and temples on their own, and at other times these efforts were undertaken in conjunction with governments, with which at times Zen was closely allied.

Despite this history, because basic Buddhism is not oriented toward social service Buddhism has been contrasted negatively with Christianity. This is the perception, but it ignores a great deal of history.

In fact, Buddhist monks throughout history were engaged in social and political issues long before contact with the West.

Beginning in the 19th century even more efforts were made to develop this side of Buddhism—in part as a result of Christian missionary activity—and make it more like traditional Christian approaches to social service.

Some of these changes were initiated by Westerners in Asia, and their efforts have been identified with a larger process of the "Protestant-ization" of Buddhism to make it more palatable to the Western, industrialized world. That said, however, many of these movements have also come from within the tradition.

Buddhism and Gender

Like Judaism, Christianity and Islam, Buddhism has traditionally been dominated by males, however it has been far more gender neutral than any of the above religions.

There have been many female Zen monks and masters in the past. Among the most famous female

Zen master was Moshan Liaoran, who died in 895. She is the only woman to have her own record in China's early *Record of the Transmission of the Lamp* anthology. She headed a male monastery and taught male students. Such a situation would be unusual even today.

Accounts of the 12th-century master Dahui's creation of the *koan* teaching method known as contemplating the critical phrase says that he honed this technique while teaching a nun called Miaodao. Dahui and some of his contemporaries taught many women, and were the first known Zen masters to leave numerous female dharma heirs.

Among the thousands of Zen masters whose biographies are recorded in later anthologies, only a few are women. A 17th-century biographer stated that men are virile and heroic, while women are gentle, passive, and weak, and incapable of meeting the rigors of the practice—a concept long taught by Western religions.

While biographies of female Zen masters were limited, large collections of poetry by women, among them many female Buddhist monks, were published during the Ming and Qing dynasties (1368-1912) in China.

There were and continue to be Zen monasteries for women in China, Japan, Korea, and Vietnam. Often these are less well supported than the male monasteries, and they have had less social and political influence. These women have been deterred by many restrictions to their avocations, but have persisted nonetheless.

Women were welcomed by Korea's Zen Buddhist orders in the kingdom of Silla in what is now Korea during the 6th and 7th centuries. In the 7th century some Silla's rulers were women—which suggests a level of equality not typical of other East Asian cultures of the time.

Buddhist women flourished in Korea until the early 15th century when the new regime made Confucianism the law of the land, gender separation was mandated and women were forbidden to become nuns.

Surviving these difficulties, orders of Korean Buddhist women continue to this day, and are the most stable and continuous of East Asian female orders. Their opportunities are nonetheless limited in comparison to those of men, particularly in the area of education.

It will take a combination of equality for women and the understanding that comes with Zen before humanity can achieve even half of its potential.

For more information about the daily life and the principles and practices of the samurai, see the author's books: *The Japanese Samurai Code* and *Samurai Strategies,* both available from Amazon.

—*Anne Frank*—
A teenage Jewish girl killed by the Nazis
during World War II after she had been hidden
in an attic for several years during which
she kept a diary that has since become
a perennial bestseller. She wrote:

"How wonderful it is
that nobody need wait
a single moment
before starting
to improve the world!"

*****